wounded
TRUST

Daring to Embrace Life at the Core of Pain

D1304611

MARY LOU YUTZY

NEW YORK

wounded TRUST
Daring to Embrace Life at the Core of Pain

© 2012 Mary Lou Yutzy. All rights reserved.

No part of this publication may be reproduced or transmitted in any form or by any means, mechanical or electronic, including photocopying and recording, or by any information storage and retrieval system, without permission in writing from author or publisher (except by a reviewer, who may quote brief passages and/or show brief video clips in a review).

Disclaimer: The Publisher and the Author make no representations or warranties with respect to the accuracy or completeness of the contents of this work and specifically disclaim all warranties, including without limitation warranties of fitness for a particular purpose. No warranty may be created or extended by sales or promotional materials. The advice and strategies contained herein may not be suitable for every situation. This work is sold with the understanding that the Publisher is not engaged in rendering legal, accounting, or other professional services. If professional assistance is required, the services of a competent professional person should be sought. Neither the Publisher nor the Author shall be liable for damages arising herefrom. The fact that an organization or website is referred to in this work as a citation and/or a potential source of further information does not mean that the Author or the Publisher endorses the information the organization or website may provide or recommendations it may make. Further, readers should be aware that internet websites listed in this work may have changed or disappeared between when this work was written and when it is read.

ISBN 978-1-61448-137-9 Paperback
ISBN 978-1-61448-138-6 eBook
Library of Congress Control Number: 2011937674

Morgan James Publishing
The Entrepreneurial Publisher
5 Penn Plaza, 23rd Floor,
New York City, New York 10001
(212) 655-5470 office • (516) 908-4496 fax
www.MorganJamesPublishing.com

Cover Photography by:
LisaKate Photography

Cover Design by:
Rachel Lopez
www.r2cdesign.com

Interior Design by:
Bonnie Bushman
bonnie@caboodlegraphics.com

In an effort to support local communities, raise awareness and funds, Morgan James Publishing donates a percentage of all book sales for the life of each book to Habitat for Humanity Peninsula and Greater Williamsburg.

Get involved today, visit
www.MorganJamesBuilds.com.

wounded TRUST

Trusting

Prov. 3:5-6

Marylu

Dedication

To the Healer of my soul: Your grace is sufficient for me.

To my loyal husband and faithful editor: you allowed me "space" to grieve though different from you. Your encouragement fueled my desire to blog and eventually write this book. Without you my words would be in the wrong order and twisted. The hours you and I spent customizing words for feelings will go down in the history of our marriage as bonding, healing, and therapeutic. Your own physical struggle with CMV in some ways mirrored my emotional seesaw and ironically helped me more clearly identify what I should be feeling. I love you to death and back!

For Kira: your "sunshine" is alive in my heart. You taught me so well when you were here with me. The loss of you has also taught me so much. Your life is alive in my heart.

Table of Contents

Foreword

Mary Lou has captured her "heart in pain" in *Wounded Trust*. You will not be able to put it down!

Many of us experience deep pain in our lives through disappointments that come in many forms, one of those being the death of a child. Her response from the beginning of her tragedy is normal to those of us who have had to say "good-bye" to our children. To think we will never see our children on this earth, or ever again, is almost more than can be comprehended.

She describes her feelings and emotions in their rawest form. I only wish I could have done the same 35 years ago when our Angela moved *home* to Heaven. I did the opposite and stuffed all of my feelings, which had devastating effects on my life and family.

This book will help to see the power of being real with God, ourselves, and others at a time when we would rather run away and hide.

Mary Lou's brutal honesty gives permission to be real. She also displays the Grace of God to you on every page of her book as she shares her intense struggle of grief.

This book will give you hope, compassion, and insight for those who hurt deeply in the face of tragedy.

Her story will help you to be patient with yourself in your grief process.

Psalms 40:1 *I waited patiently for the Lord; He turned to me and heard my cry.*

This book will encourage you to cry out to the Lord, not once, not twice, but as often as you need. He will ALWAYS meet you with grace and strength; enough for the moment.

Her courage to write her story is a gift to all of us who grieve.

Anne Beiler

Founder of Auntie Anne's pretzels

Author and speaker

THE KNIFE

The knife came out of nowhere. Jagged, ugly, and dull, it cut through the skin in a very unskilled manner. Blood spurted out as it sliced down through the skin. Knocked over by the blow, I was emotionally stunned and wounded badly. Shock took over; the realities of life seemed small in comparison with what really mattered. Clearly I needed tender loving care, sympathy, and someone to walk beside me holding me up, because I was too weak to stand. Still it had to be my choice to want help, to feel God, and to let others bring aid.

Grief placed me into this process. The knife of loss literally opened my heart. I feel sliced open, vulnerable. I am wounded and just functioning from day to day, hour-to-hour, and minute-to-minute. The blessing of shock makes me only recognize what is important today. Next week, next month, next year, or in twenty years is hidden from sight. The pain is too great to face in reality. The knife of grief is sharp and intense. I need God like never before in my life, but strangely He felt far away. Shock usually portrays a strong sense of needing help. I am desperate for someone to notice that I need help to function from day to day. Someone to bring sense out of this stupor that has engulfed me. The pain is overwhelming and tears are raining down.

CHAPTER ONE

the wound

February 18th started just like any other day. I was a busy mother of three little girls I enjoyed to the fullest. Marlea was five, Kira had just turned three, and Anna was ten months old. Life was good, although quite different from what I had dreamed of in being a single, independent nurse in a far-off land.

Merlin and I met and fell in love at age 18, just two years after all my prophetic statements regarding my lofty dreams. In June of 2000 we exchanged marriage vows. Merlin was just out of college, so we became resident innkeepers at Olde Homestead Suites, a small bed & breakfast in Lancaster County, Pennsylvania. We planned to stay approximately two years, and then move on to raising a family. Merlin also worked another job, so we were very busy. We fell in love with the people and the B&B atmosphere. Having three children and running a B&B left rare dull moments. 2008 came and we still had not moved elsewhere.

We had just come through several busy days following the death and funeral of my aunt. After spending time with family and living on the go, down time at home sounded inviting. The girls had the flu and I was lacking sleep. Toward Wednesday afternoon I noticed Kira was getting fussy. She was past taking naps but I figured since she had been sick she probably needed to sleep. I rocked her to sleep, and she slept for two hours. I was a bit worried; my motherly instinct told me to be watchful, so I was carefully observant. Kira was abnormally quiet that evening and went to bed early. Around midnight I heard her stirring. I was sure she was going to throw up, so Merlin ran for her. Sure enough, I was right. "Oh no, not this again" I thought to myself.

Merlin slept with Kira so I could get some rest. She was up two more times throwing up. Around four we gave her a bath and she seemed really "out of it." I knew she had to be extremely tired so I wasn't too worried. By six a.m. she had the dry heaves and I still wasn't too worried. My children often went through that when they were sick. She seemed to have a fever and Merlin and I tried to keep Tylenol in her. I got up at nine, by which time Merlin had come home from an appointment and was ready for breakfast. He carried Kira to the recliner and she gave him a kiss before he left again.

I noticed Kira's breathing was ragged, so I quickly tried to feed my screaming baby before calling the doctor. When Kira started dry heaving again I went over to her. This time she didn't get her breath again and turned blue. Panic seized me. I was terrified. I grabbed her, screaming at the top of my lungs, and ran for the bathroom. Adrenaline taking over, I yelled for Marlea to get the phone. Ten years earlier I had taken my last CPR class. As my mind raced, the CPR procedure came back to me. "God" I screamed "I never wanted to do this on my own child." This wasn't why I learned CPR. I managed to dial 911 between CPR and yelled at the operator to help me keep going. Marlea was terrified and Anna was screaming on her high chair. Marlea ran next door and got a friend who worked for us; she came in to our apartment and took care of the children. Somehow I managed to keep doing mouth to mouth to Kira, give our address to the operator, and meanwhile giving Marlea instructions. My heart was dying; this was too ugly to be true.

Three minutes later the door burst open and two neighbors, Sylvan and Sam, ran inside. Sam was carrying a first responder's bag. I didn't know him very well and didn't realize he was an EMT. He had heard the call on the scanner and came running. We continued CPR together. I was still horrified and frightened, but his presence and ability were gifts from God. I hung up the phone, even managed to say thanks to the operator, another one of my angels, as I would realize later. The ambulance arrived eight minutes after I had placed the call, another miracle for which we were thankful.

Inside of me my heart was full of disbelief and anger. I was already on the path of guilt and blaming myself, and anger was pouring out of me toward God. As the paramedics put her on the board and tried more reviving methods I called my sister, Renita. "Kira is dying" I yelled and hung up. Merlin ran in soon after that. The look of mixed terror and horror on his face when he saw Kira will stay with me until heaven. Kira still wasn't responding. I heard the word "transport." They practically ran out the door with her. I could feel their anxiety growing even though they were trying hard to stay calm. I ran behind them throwing their bags into the back of the ambulance. Merlin jumped into the front of the ambulance to go with them to the hospital. I stayed at home to eat my breakfast and feed Anna before going to the hospital. My heart felt dead as I walked back to our front door; the ambulance was already out the driveway and down the road. As the front door banged shut behind me I realized in my horrible state that I had choices to make. I felt determination rising inside of me. I was going to somehow stay alive even if Kira didn't.

So I yelled. Anita, a friend and neighbor, came in and we yelled together. We yelled at the top of our lungs; mostly at God, and somewhat at circumstances while I chided myself for not being worried sooner. I went to the bedroom and tried to put on my shoes. Anita was praying in between my yelling. Sylvan came back in also and prayed with me. Yelling felt good because I was being real. That's what my heart was doing too, yelling with all it's might. The desire to stay present in my pain was real and was the first good choice I made. A peace came over me and denial left me. I was expecting the phone to ring and hear someone saying that Kira was gone. My parents came and took me to the hospital. They were still in shock, not realizing how bad the situation actually was. Every time their phone rang I curled into a fetal position.

We walked into the emergency room at Lancaster General Hospital expecting to not recognize anyone and for someone to tell me that Kira is gone. God knew what I needed better than I and had my oldest brother, Arlin, and a cousin waiting for me. My cousin, Sandy, informed me that Kira was still alive and Tim (her husband and a specialist at LGH) was back in trauma with her. Trauma; the word cut me to the bone. I never wanted to go in there. I felt dazed as I walked through the maze of nurse stations, curtains, and eyes. The last curtain appeared in front of me and I heard the familiar voice of Merlin talking to Kira. I was so happy when I saw Kira because she was pink again. I felt myself relax and a tiny bit of hope grew inside me. Merlin was beside Kira and the staff encouraged us to keep talking to her although she still was not responding. The hope that I felt was cruel. Simply hope that doctors, hospital, and medicine could perform some kind of miracle for our little girl. I wanted her life back, and for everything to be okay. This was way out of my comfort zone. Life Flight soon flew Kira to Hershey Medical Center, an excellent area hospital specializing in pediatric care.

Over the next five days the doctors, nurses, and we parents fought for her life. Kira remained unconscious with no sign of life. It would have been nice to believe that there was a twitch, an eyelid flicker, a finger moving. Other than her chest rising and falling because of the machines, no signs of life came, just stillness. Sleepless nights, intense grief, and vacillating feelings all became a part of us. The memories also became part of us, the good along with the bad. My choice to embrace the pain and stay present continued in the hospital and also became part of my life. It also helped those around us not be on tiptoes but to embrace the pain also.

That night on the way home with my parents, Satan came to me. The experience was horrible. I knew I was sitting on the seat of this car but bodily I felt as if I was being pulled down into a pit. Though not physically, I clawed trying to keep out of it. But the torment continued to pull me down, down, down. Lies, lots of them. Hopelessness and despair. "Your fault, your fault, your fault" the walls of the pit seemed to echo around me.

The more I believed it the darker the pit became. I heard echoing laughter "You believed you were such a good mom and look what happened to you." Hideous laughs. "What will you do with this…you are going to go down. I cried out to God aloud and to my earthly father in the driver's seat. I was weak; too weak to even mention the name of Jesus. My father was not weak and at the sound of his voice and the name of Jesus, Satan left, although his torment did not. I was drained physically, emotionally, and spiritually. The thought that he would prey on me made me angry. It also made me realize that I needed to claim the blood of Jesus and His grace. Earlier as we left the hospital I called two of Merlin's friends. Dan was already packing his bags to leave for the hospital. Dave also appeared in short order. Merlin went through the same attack later on in the night at the hospital. Dan and Dave were with him and prayed against Satan. That night's experience established more firmly in my mind the protection we have over our children. Kira was walking through the valley of the shadow of death. That is what it felt like to us also. The peace God gave was so real in that valley.

That night was a tough one for Kira, and by morning it appeared evident that even with life support, she wouldn't live much longer. Merlin and Ana, a friend and cousin, had taken turns beside her during the night. The day was a blur of trying to figure out what had happened and how. Ana is also an RN, so she and Tim were part of our doctor consultations. Having someone with medical knowledge explain things to us after the doctor left was extremely valuable. The tests came back negative except for the one done at Lancaster General Hospital. Bacteria was growing, a gram-negative rod, but the strain of the bacteria was still unknown. I sat heartbroken, racking my brain for any possible thing that might have set off the bacteria. It was horrible. I felt so low and like the world's most neglectful mother. The blame I felt inside of me was strong. That afternoon I spent some time with the Pediatric Intensive Care Unit counselor. My sister Renita sat with me. The counselor's words of truth were like gold to me. When I could grasp the hope of the cross, when I realized that it could cover even a horrid mother, when I believed that it didn't matter what the burden was at the foot of the cross, when I could feel in my heart that Jesus is always there at the cross, I made my second most important decision. I chose that no matter if Kira lived or died, I would stay at the foot of the cross. Jesus is always there.

On Friday morning Merlin's brothers came from Ohio to be with us. Their support and presence made a huge difference especially for Merlin. Later on that night my two sisters, Edith and Evelyn also came. Merlin's parents also came to give support. Having family beside us was a gift that we appreciated very much.

By Saturday night we were close to receiving a diagnosis. HIB is an abbreviation for Haemophilus Influenza type B. It typically comes as a secondary infection, with pneumonia for an example. In Kira's case, HIB was the primary infection, resulting in bacteria crossing the blood-brain barrier; in other words, meningitis (inflammation of the meninges, the area around the brain and spinal cord.) This diagnosis took quite some time for me to process. Slowly I began to realize the reason I didn't know she was sick was because Kira didn't even know. Neither did she feel any pain; never did her brain know what was going on. Being only three and not having a large vocabulary, Kira didn't even know how a headache felt, much less to be able to tell me. The feelings of condemnation began to slowly leave me. The doctor's words of truth began to replace the doubt I felt inside. Through my daze I heard the words "unavoidable," "if you would have brought her the night before we would probably still have the same outcome," "you did your best," "you are amazing," "this bacteria was too strong for any drug," and "germs are always ahead of the scientist." The ugly truth of nothing having made a difference was hard to accept. Kira had vaccinations at four months, including the HIB vaccine, but did not receive an 18-month booster shot. However, no booster shots were available over this time, since the vaccinations had been recalled for sterility issues.

Saturday night I spent the night with Kira. Her heart was doing gallops, consisting of the heart rate climbing quickly and dropping erratically. An adult in this condition lasts about five minutes. Kira went on for hours. I sat beside her in pain, realizing any minute could be her last. My sister Edith sat with me. About three a.m. the nurses came to suction her lungs. When they were finished, her heart rate suddenly dropped back to 150 and stayed there. It felt like a miracle, and I was elated. After being on pins and needles for hours I was finally able to relax a bit the rest of the night.

Sunday was our most hopeful day. We watched closely for more changes, and maybe even imagined some changes. Merlin and I spent some time talking about the coming days and the decisions that might possibly lie ahead of us. We were both exhausted; the pain of watching our little girl lie there so still and unresponsive was taking its toll on our bodies. It was heartbreaking to watch Merlin wish to rescue his child and remain unable to physically do anything. Doubly heartbreaking was Marlea; she was completely devastated. We allowed her to go back and talk with Kira and sit beside her when she would come for her daily visit.

Our family and friends were very supportive. Church friends came every day, organized and managed a meal schedule, and made sure everything functioned smoothly. They even brought meals for us and those with us at the hospital. We ate, functioned, laughed, and cried. Cousin Tim came all the way from Texas. The reminiscing from childhood days eased the reality and strengthened me. Other friends came and went each day, leaving their love and encouragement with us. Many of them went back to Kira and sat with her for a few minutes with Merlin or me. Lydia, a close friend and cousin, wondered what she could do. I said, "Just come and be with me," so she did. Renita, Ana, Lydia, and I sat together talking and crying. They heard my anguish, argued with me about the blame, and stood beside me praying and fighting for my sanity.

But no one, no circumstance, and no story could take away the pain. My entire body felt as if a knife were cutting away everything that mattered in life and in how our lives functioned from day to day. Excruciating pain filled me. The knife seared deep into the core of my soul. My muscles reacted, my heart reacted, and my brain raced. Again and again I gave this pain to Jesus and felt a calming peace. In turn, I was able to laugh a little amid the tears and also embrace the reality before me. Being able to stay present in the midst of deep pain was powerful at that moment and also even now.

Monday came with more big decisions and more tests. Hoping for Kira's survival did not seem possible any longer; what hope existed was rapidly fading. All the tests came back the same, showing no brain activity. We began to feel the stark reality of all hope being snatched away and to realize that healing doesn't always mean earthly healing. That realization felt cold and ugly; and yet heaven felt so close, and distinctly warm and inviting for Kira. The suffering her body was going through was clear. Our prayer for her to live life fully, here or in heaven was strong.

Monday night I stayed at the hospital again. Edith, Matt (Merlin's brother), Merlin, and I sat around her bedside late into the night. Most of the time we spent telling stories and laughing. Some of the stories were about her; some were just funny ones from years ago. It felt so right to be silly just like her. I spent the rest of the night nestled close beside her, treasuring the hours left with her. I felt paralyzed by the pain, scared, and more fearful than I had ever been in my life. Sorrow overwhelmed me as I cried and cried. By four in the morning my fear was escalating even more. About that time I heard the door open and Renita's husband, Paul walked in. He didn't have much to say, just sat there praying for several hours. It gave me strength and peace to know that I was not alone.

Tuesday morning came and with it reality. As Merlin and I faced each other in the privacy of a room for parents in our situation, no words were necessary to say what needed to be said. Who would have thought that sometime we would be faced with a decision such as this? Merlin was beginning to feel that we should let her go peacefully. The reality that no brain activity was observed seemed stark and foreboding. Making her body suffer any longer seemed so wrong. I felt so weak, wanting to hold onto false hopes. I wanted to run away, jump out a window, and never come back. Gently Merlin kept pulling me back to reality and to the fact that I could be strong and we could do what was right for her, even though it meant our earthly loss.

The day passed quickly. Evening came and with it the reality of telling Marlea that her sister was going to die. Together we wailed and cried. Later we walked again down the foreboding hallway to PICU with Marlea so that she could say good-bye to Kira. We read out of Kira's favorite book - *Curious George*. Marlea picked the story about George being the Man with the Yellow Hat's Christmas present, ending with them both riding off in a carriage. Marlea's choice made so much sense to me, just like Kira was going to ride off with Jesus in a carriage. Then Marlea started singing. She sang and sang to the little sister her own made-up song about heaven. It went on and on. I sat behind Marlea weeping and Merlin sat beside us.

Later that evening, as I lay in bed holding my daughter as her heart beat its last, I faced the worst fear a mother can face. We sang lots of songs and prayed for what seemed like hours. Our parents, most of our siblings, and a few friends were in the room with us, surrounded us with patience and entered into our grief. The agony was overwhelming. Finally, with no more excuses or songs we told the doctor to turn off the machine. On February 24, 2009 Kira Mary Yutzy peacefully slipped from this life into the next.

Hours later, around midnight, we stumbled over the threshold of our front door exhausted and in the deepest sorrow known to any human. With us was a five-year-old girl whose sorrow was deeper than our own, and a ten-month-old who was, thankfully, oblivious. We had a snack by the fireplace. It was cozy, and the snack was a big basket of food from friends; but the room felt cold and empty without our sunshine girl.

Still hours later sleep evaded me. It was now around three a.m. I sneaked back to the girls' room. Merlin was sleeping with Marlea to ease the pain of Kira not being in bed with her. They were both peacefully asleep. I crept closer and found tears on my husband's face. He was fast asleep but the tears were still coming freely. And thus began our journey of pain and grief.

CHAPTER TWO

pain

To feel pain is to feel the beginning of healing.

The Lord is nigh unto them that are of a broken heart; and saveth such as be of a contrite spirit. **Psalm 34:18**

Pain, pain, pain… our lives are full of it. Everywhere I turn, pain follows me. I try to run away; it follows me closely. I run faster and find I cannot leave it behind. I try to pretend it belongs to someone else; no others have the capacity or circumstances to receive my pain. I try to give it away, but no one wants this pain I have to offer. This pain is mine to keep, embrace, and fully endure.

Every morning I slowly wake up. The pain greets me bitterly. I heave a sigh. Do I really have to live another day like this? I sit up and gradually get my feet to the floor. Numbly I walk to the bathroom. Yes, same face, same swollen eyes, same drained-looking skin. I don't even know the person I see in the mirror. Where is that other one I used to see? "God" I scream, "I still wanted to be her. I don't want to be this person. She is someone different. You never told me you were going to change me this way. You didn't ask. I never gave permission." Sheer terror fills my heart as I realize that I have to get dressed and act as if I didn't die, even though my heart feels dead. The pain is too much for me; my eyes and body give way to tears. Not only do I have this pain, but so do my little girl, my baby, and my husband. Today I will have to watch our five-year-old try to function without her sidekick. Today no one will call Kira for breakfast, lunch, or supper. Today again we will have an empty place at the table. Today again no one will want to set the table; the act is simply too painful. We all have our own dose and it's all unique and different, because we are all different people and all loved Kira differently.

Yesterday was Sunday and we went to church, our first time without Kira. We couldn't get ourselves out of bed, so we didn't arrive until almost eleven, two hours late. Even the chair left for me seemed cold and cruel. The fleeting looks of the people around me also broke my heart. I am different; I am looked at differently, and yes, I look different. The pain, the experiences of the last several days have changed me. I have said things that I never said before. I wept in front of people, as I had never done before. Never before have I met my emotional bottom in a public experience like the funeral brought.

Never had I said good-bye to my baby before. It was always "hello, welcome to this world." We don't expect our children to die; we expect to die before them. To experience our own child's death is the wrong way to the grave. My body is very aware of that truth but my brain and heart are still in shock. My mind drifts further, to the day before yesterday, out at the graveside. I thought I would be okay. I thought I had said my good-bye when I heard that lid snap shut on the casket. But when pallbearers lowered the casket into the grave my whole body rebelled. I had more body pain than I knew was possible to experience. The day had been cold and damp, and now my body was full of muscle cramps. Nothing took them away; they had only intensified as I heard and saw the shovelfuls of dirt falling on her casket.

I jerk back to reality again as the preacher closes this morning's service. I want to run away again. I don't want to talk to anyone or have anyone act as if I am even close to normal. Marlea clings to my skirt, also trying to get away from the pain. Later in the afternoon reality starts to sink in as my sisters' and Merlin's family leave to return to Ohio. As I watch them go I can't help but be a little jealous. Too bad I can't just go away too. But no, this pain is mine to endure. They promise their prayers and thoughts. I know they loved Kira too and feel the pain, although not to the same extent.

My daze ends and I realize I am still staring into the mirror. The person staring back at me is the person feeling all this pain. This is who I am now. This is how my days will probably be for the next year at least, maybe more. I have no idea. Mysterious as well, is how this pain will affect me and my little family. As different as I feel already…I feel my heart preparing for more changes, unpredictable circumstances, and days of confusion and darkness.

I phase out again remembering what several people told me at the viewing. "We will pray for patience for you." Patience, why that? I pondered that statement. Two days later I already am beginning to understand. Yes, this does take patience. Patience with myself, patience with my husband, and patience with my children. In reality we feel the gap in age so strongly in our little family with five years between Marlea and Anna. The pain of that gap will always be there, but we will be able to somewhat adjust to it. The thought strikes me that Marlea will be 21 when Anna turns 16. Marlea especially will feel the gap the rest of her life with the loss of her playmate and best friend. She doesn't like to play alone or even be alone, since Kira was a soul mate to her. That in itself will take patience for me as I help her adjust. During the last six months especially they were together all the time. The pain of being without Kira is intensified when we see Marlea alone, lonely, and trying to sort out life. Yesterday I was crying and she came and sat on my lap, rubbed my arm, and said, "It's okay Mommy, Kira is with Jesus." Somewhere in all this pain and lonely emotions God has a special arrangement for little children.

Well, I need patience right now to comb my hair because I think they too have changed. Oh dear, is my hair responding to pain too? I jerk it just to make sure that I can still feel it. I can. Anger comes with the jerk. I slam my comb down on the counter in exasperation. There are too many feelings coming my way. I can't decipher them. What brain cells are left remind me that this too is part of pain. The five stages of grief: isolation and denial, anger, bargaining, depression, and acceptance are already a part of my life. My organized mind expected them to be neatly in order, and I could predict or even pick which one I would experience presently. Grief is not like that. It is not organized and seems to have no predictable sequence. I already feel all these stages jumbling together; I am confused. I just got out of bed and started the first week. A feeling of powerlessness and lack of control comes over me. Overwhelmed, I think the right thing for me to do is to simply go back to bed, pull the covers over my head, and isolate myself from the rest of the world. But no, that would be following the grief stages so I should counteract them with something.

Vaguely I remember my vow to remain present in this experience. If I live today and just let all these feelings come maybe I can "get over it" faster. I realize it's a wrong motive, but this pain drives me to try. My determination to live wholly comes back to me. I am glad for this pain; it means I can still feel. The gift of this pain means I loved Kira, cared for her, and was a good mom. It also means I am still alive to care for the rest of my family. For that I am grateful. This raw feeling is something God gave for me to choose what to do with it.

I will not run away from this pain. It is mine. With this gift of pain I will heal. This journey is not for me alone. This journey is one Jesus knows well. No one except Jesus wants my pain. He opens His arms wide and I give my pain to Him again daily, hourly, and moment by moment. I can't feel Him, but I read in my Bible that He is close to the broken-hearted; I believe that describes me, Marlea, Merlin, and even little Anna. Broken-hearted, sliced open as with a knife, exposing our core. To feel pain means we can choose to trust Jesus to heal us, to bind up our wounds, restore our trust in Him again. We will be the same people, but we will never the same. I will never look in the mirror again and see the person I saw in this mirror two weeks ago. She is gone, and will not return. She will live on in my mind and sometimes I will fantasize what it would be like to be her, but never in reality. Even the simplicity of a child's pain and grief has a way of drawing me close to the Father, making me realize how accessible His grace is in my daily life. Together Jesus and I will walk this road of pain. Sometimes I will need to be reminded, and other times He will carry me. There is nothing that I will feel that He will not know about already.

I finish my waking up and feel refreshed. Thankful for Someone to walk with me. Thankful that I am not alone. Thankful for God who gives me the ability to be determined to feel, to have the courage to face circumstances. Above all thankful for God, who with pain will give grace, patience, and healing. I can face this day and the coming days. I will open my eyes every morning and be greeted by pain again. Along with this pain I will choose daily to walk with Jesus and feel His grace in my life. My lifeline will not come from whether or not I am remembered in my pain. My lifeline will come from my heavenly Father who never forgets and never wearies of my tears. The pain is part of my life and that will have to be okay. Somewhere in this jumble I will still laugh, rejoice, crack jokes, and have fun with my children. In this pileup of feelings I purpose in my heart to not run from this pain, this gift. In the deepest times of despair when I want to isolate myself from Merlin and others I will refuse. I will instead follow that still small voice down in the bottom corner of my heart. It is whispery quiet but I still hear it. I will follow the still small voice of God. He will guide me through this pain to wholeness and real joy again. My wounded heart will sometime trust freely and wholly again.

For now, breakfast time is here. Little girls need to wake up. More cards will arrive to be opened today, and more flowers will greet us at our door. Guests will arrive to check in, and a life that is still meant to be lived can be enjoyed today.

CHAPTER THREE

separation

The place at which diversion or parting occurs

Jesus wept **John 11:35**

We feel separation intensely, daily, every minute. We are separated from Kira for the rest of our time here on earth. This separation feels like a wall. It's a wall that I would like to tear through and abolish. It is gigantic, stretching between earth and heaven. It makes me angry and sad all at the same time. I don't want to be separated; I want my daughter. It's not a bad dream; it's real. I have only been separated from her for four weeks. This is how the rest of my life here on earth will be, separated from her.

We will live, grow older, change. She will not change with us. We will never see her as a teenager, young woman, or mother. We will always try to picture what she would be like now. How tall she would be, what color her hair would shine, whether or not she would have crooked teeth, how much she would weigh, and what size shoe she would wear. We will try to imagine if Marlea's dresses would fit her now, if she would be as tall as her big sister. What if she would need glasses? Would she tend to play with Marlea or play more with Anna? Would she mind going to the dentist? Would she still like animals? Would the clothes she picks out match or would she want to wear them because of how they feel? Perhaps she would like to wear tights in the wintertime. How old would she be when she would meet her match? Or perhaps she would be a globetrotter or career woman and never marry. If she would marry, what would her children be like? Would she still be as energetic and crazy as a teenager and mother as she was as a three-year-old child?

But the wall is there; we will never know here what all goes on in heaven. Do residents change there or do they stay the same? God made us to grow and mature to beauty. Do they stop growing when they reach that prime age in heaven? Mysteries and imaginations are all that our brains can explore; we are separated. We will always wonder what she looks like in heaven and we will never know until we get there. My arrival could be tomorrow, next year, thirty, or even fifty years. I don't know. Separation could go on and on for what seems like a long time to us. But, to Kira, a thousand years could seem very brief indeed. My human mind can't fathom that.

My mother heart wants to reach out and touch her. I can't; I am on earth and she in heaven. I want to hold her hand, run my hand through her fine, silky hair. I want to make her breakfast, put on her shoes and coat. I can't since she doesn't need them. I want to care for her when she is sick, cold, or lonely. She never needs my physical help any longer. I want to her to run toward me, into my arms and give me a sound smoochy kiss. I can't because she is no longer mine. I beg God for another chance, to know about HIB and do it over. I can't, for she is already gone.

Death feels final and forever to us on earth, the only thing that can be this life changing. Death can steal a normal day and turn it into a worst nightmare. Separation is brought by death. Heaven is a place beyond compare and defying description; I plan to go. The only thing that really matters to me is whether or not people go to heaven. I don't want anyone to miss it. The feeling burns inside me with the terrible separation that I am experiencing. The thought of enduring separation forever makes me want to go out and shout and encourage all people to not miss their chance, to not waste their lives, to live fully and purposefully while on earth. Having been separated from a dear companion is terrible to experience, but even much more so is to think of eternal separation from God. Being at heaven's gates, wanting to enter but instead being sent to hell makes me shudder. This separation, and enduring this unseen wall is enough torture for me.

Last night we were again feeling terribly sad, on a Friday night, which is usually family night. Here came the weekend and memories of all the fun family time we used to have. The pain of separation, and longing for Kira, God, and heaven; also crying out for comfort to our Heavenly Father. Night, when everything is dark and still, God seems so close to us. As I lay in my bed weeping, the ceiling seemed to open above me. My heavenly Father appeared to me in a vision. With open outstretched arms He whispered these words "Come child, I weep with you. But My grace is enough for anything." The comfort that enveloped me drifted into my body and brain, and I was soon asleep.

"Children of the heavenly Father, safely in His bosom gather,
nesting bird nor star in heaven, such a refuge ere was given.
For He giveth or He taketh, God his children ne'er forsaketh,
tis the loving purpose solely to preserve them pure and holy.
Neither life nor death shall ever, from the Lord his children sever,
unto them His grace He showeth and their sorrows all He knoweth."
—in a hymn penned by Lina Sandell

CHAPTER FOUR

to love a child

Charity suffereth long, and is kind; charity envieth not; charity vaunteth not itself, is not puffed up, Doth not behave itself unseemly, seeketh not her own, is not easily provoked, thinketh no evil; Rejoiceth not in iniquity, but rejoiceth in the truth; Beareth all things, *believeth all things, hopeth all things, endureth all things.* **1 Corinthians 13:4-7**

When a mother gives birth to a child, a part of her is never the same again. A mother chooses to love, to care for this child that God has given. Love is a dare. Dare to love well and unconditionally. Dare to love even when it will hurt. Dare to love even though life is unpredictable. Dare to love when it could be taken away. Dare to love when you have no true idea of who this child will be. Dare to love even when the cute baby stage is over. Dare to promise to love forever!

Kira's birth was fairly dramatic for us. Marlea had to be convinced to come out a week after her due date. Because of that we had no idea what to expect. All I knew was that I was very tired of being pregnant. The night before Kira's birth I ran up and down stairs, did jumping jacks, and sat in a Jacuzzi for a while. We made a party out of it, and included Marlea. We went to the hospital around nine the next morning. Merlin, true to his inborn mechanic spirit needed to drop off a truck at a nearby shop, meaning

I needed to carry out my own suitcase, drive the car to the shop, and then proceed to the hospital. Both of us have gotten some good laughs from the experience. Driving while in labor was quite interesting.

Kira Mary 2 months old

Kira was born that afternoon at 2:45. Merlin held her first, and I thought they were never going to get finished talking to each other. I watched in amazement as they bonded. They understood each other ever after that like only a father and daughter can. This was the second girl for Merlin, and he now was comfortable being a father. Together we loved her, cared for her, and met her needs. She was sweet, innocent, and joyful. Marlea and I sang "You are my Sunshine, my only Sunshine, you make me happy when skies are gray…." She brought us sunshine. Marlea spent hours entertaining her for me and keeping Kira happy.

Before we had Kira, I had a miscarriage around eight weeks of pregnancy. I was devastated. To make matters worse, two of my sisters were expecting babies a week before and a week after me. In the end, the miscarriage was a good experience for me. I learned to appreciate the life God gives. I don't naturally appreciate changes. Marlea's birth was a big change for me. I went from working six days a week to taking care of a fussy little bundle. I juggled the baby and work and struggled keeping a positive attitude toward children. I wanted Marlea and loved her but saw her too much as an interruption to my work. The miscarriage changed that for me. I vowed to never again complain about children, no matter what.

Kira was born a year after the miscarriage experience. I would soon find out what vows mean. She was a good baby up until about five to six months old. From that point on until she turned two she would wake up at night and often be awake for two to three hours. Many a night as I sat rocking her half-dazed I would think of my vow. Complaining wasn't an option! Instead I held her closer and thanked God for her. I spent a lot more time with her this way than I would have had she been sleeping. As a result, Merlin's and my heart bonded with her to a very strong degree. Merlin also spent many hours with her. We tried lots of different things, avoided some foods for a while, etc. but nothing seemed to really help. Soon after her second birthday we all made some diet changes which she apparently liked, because that was the end of her nighttime episodes.

Only recently did I realize that her name actually means "a form of the sun." The one thing Merlin and I both keep realizing time and again is how we loved her so well. She wasn't an easy child; she was extremely energetic and many times drove our nerves over the edge. The dare to love this child was so real to us because she complicated it very well. One of Merlin's pet peeves is when children shriek or use a very shrill voice. His ears do not appreciate high frequencies at all. Well, Kira loved to shriek. She did it at inappropriate times; in the car, at church, or at the table. She loved to "push that button." Some sense of satisfaction was evident. After we bought her a leopard coat, we called Kira "the screaming leopard." No form of punishment could squelch the sheer pleasure she got out of that terrible habit. Over the time her habit was really bad, in church one night she let out one crazily loud shriek. I was mortified. The speaker soon interjected "I enjoy hearing children make noise. A child that hears will make noise. Three of our children are deaf. The ability to make noise is a gift from God that we often take for granted." Screamer or not, she was Kira, she was ours, and we loved her… Dare to love when it's unpredictable.

In the hospital, as I held her and gave her back to Jesus on February 24, I was able to say with all my heart "God, here is Kira; I give her back to You. Thanks for letting me love her and care for her. You enabled me to love her well. I learned a lot from her in her birth, her life, and now her death. I now give her back to you, well-loved." I think of this so often, and the miracle of having no regrets in loving her. If giving our child back to God is this difficult, how hard it must really be for God to have given her to us. I knew when I gave Kira back to Him that He will care for her needs to the utmost. He knew I couldn't be perfect. He knew I would make mistakes. He knew I would be embarrassed by her shrieks in church. He knew I would not like to stay up at night with her night after night. He knew I would be tempted to complain. He knew I would sometimes misread her and become exasperated at her. Yet He gave her to us anyway. He didn't require perfection of me and even left me to freely make my own choices and mistakes. I feel so honored to be trusted by a God who trusts me even in my human-ness.

This fifth week has been extremely hard for us. I am physically and emotionally exhausted. Tuesday Merlin was sick and we ended up in the ER at LGH for several hours. They gave him fluids, pain medication, and oxygen, and discharged him; for which we were thankful. We were not looking forward to a hospital stay! We spent the next several hours with Merlin's doctor, and were quite thankful for his input. Merlin apparently had a blocked stomach. He has been getting better although still is not back to normal. Whatever is normal!? It's hard to be okay with one's emotional state and also experience physical pain. Merlin's stomach is better, but yet he isn't better. This time of the year always causes his CMV virus to flare up, so it's hard to know what the problem really is. Marlea wasn't feeling very well again and I spent Wednesday on the couch also. Marlea and Anna have been awake sometimes at night. I am lacking sleep.

It was really hard for us to be back at Lancaster General Hospital again. The good thing was that one of the nurses that took care of Kira came and talked with me. We had not thought much about LGH and our feelings from being there. I was scared to go to LGH again, and felt like I was reliving Kira's illness in some ways while also dealing with trying not to be too frightened about Merlin. I relived the terror I felt walking into the ER expecting Kira to not be living anymore and the hope I felt after I saw her color. The dare to hope for life that we felt and then in the end to give her to Jesus for life in heaven was so real, and yet so unreal. Reliving that part of our experience was so confusing and heart wrenching again.

The past several nights' dreams would cause me to wake up full of hope only to realize that they were not true. The valley of denial, grief, anger, and shock feels as if it has started all over again. I say this because I feel weak, worn, and battered. I cry out to Him again and again in anguish, my mother heart full of pain and loneliness for Kira. I am human, with a human mind, and I can't see or know His whole plan for us, for Marlea, and for Anna. Again, because He has shown me without a doubt that He is God, I choose to trust my heavenly Father who loves me and gave His own Son for me.

CHAPTER FIVE

kira—
who she was

A Tribute to Kira—By Her Daddy
God sends His love to us
In many ways it's shown
Three years ago it was a girl
As Kira she was known

It was not long until we knew
We had a special child
Kira quickly grew and really soon
She was on her feet, running wild

Soon after that she learned quite well
Dad's time was spent across the street
And any chance she had she'd try
To catch up to her daddy's feet

Kira's fingers found a way
To cinch her daddy's heart
And though one tenth his age
As friends like this, how can we part?

Her cherub smile and winsome gaze
Found ways into many a heart
Though she'll not come back, we know
Memories of Kira will not depart

Then stumbling through a maze of confusion
We seek to claim God's healing grace
In life, we'll find enough to go on
In heaven, doubts flee when seeing His face!

So briefly lay down your cares and remember
God's time is not your own, you see
Give loved ones a hug or tender kiss
Doing so will continue the legacy of Kiki

I feel Jesus' tears falling on me as I bow in sorrow at the foot of the cross. My loss is great… my treasure is in heaven and tonight I am unable to go there to retrieve it.

Kira, meaning "light/sun" was born on February 6, 2006. We were absolutely thrilled to have another little girl. Marlea was quite protective and loved her right away. She didn't stay little for long at all.

By the time she was six weeks old she looked more like a three-month-old. Figuring out that she was going to be tall and aggressive didn't take long either. By five months she was sliding out of our laps and onto the floor to roll to where she wanted to go, which was usually Marlea's dollhouse. She would roll all over the floor and was soon sliding and wiggling like a little snake all over the house. Her clothes were dirty from the tip of her chin down to her toes. She filled our lives with joy and sunshine.

Her main object in life soon became well known: going outside. Anytime the door opened she was right there. At eight months old she had mastered going up and down stairs with ease. Once, I finally found her upstairs in the inn exploring the hallway after a quick frantic search. She had somehow pried open the unlatched door and was off to explore. Napping was a waste of time, she thought, and so fought naps as much as she possibly could. Some days if I was lucky, Merlin would take her for a ride on the mower and upon return she would be asleep. Kira became a nightmare to watch closely after she began to walk. We live right by a state route plus have a parking lot for the inn just outside our front door. I had to constantly be right with her, otherwise fearing an accident. When I mowed yard, her favorite dare was seeing how close she could get to the road until I ran for her. It frightened me terribly and she knew it.

Once I found her in the store next door just looking to see what she could find. I would turn my back for a minute and she would be gone. One morning I went outside and found Kira was already there, playing. After that, we put chains on the doors not to keep people out, but to keep the little people where they were supposed to stay. She was so tall that opening doors and reaching up into drawers or onto tabletops were no problem at all. She loved to push the stroller, not ride in it. Why would you ride when you can drive?

In church, why would one be quiet when screaming was possible? By the time Kira was two she had calmed down a lot; she and Marlea were playing together more. Marlea patiently taught her to play doll and dollhouse. They had lots of fights and lots of fun. We learned quickly to keep Kira's fingernails trimmed, because they were her weapons. Kira had plenty excess energy and could easily keep up with Marlea. One of my favorite memories was one

night last summer when she pushed (ran) the Little Tykes shopping cart up and down a well-sloped hill again and again, just for fun.

When Anna was born, Kira was so helpful. She was always the first to run when Anna cried. She drove us nuts sometimes, but I always said she will be a good mother. She loved to play jail and would say "Put you in jail; whole house jail." Sometimes she would put chairs around me in the kitchen and declare me to be in jail. Kira was also very softhearted and sometimes sweetly shy. She was

an early riser and would often wake up the other two. She called herself by her daddy's nickname for her "Kiki" up until the last week. Then she proudly said "Kir-da." She was my little helper, and often cleaned out the dishwasher for me, helped with wash, tried to mow lawn, and helped operate the sweeper. She had just started going to Sunday school and was so proud of it. She was becoming a little lady and was so beautiful. We discovered she had grown three inches again in the last three months. She was easily headed to being over six feet tall. The troubles of life were just starting to bother her. Whenever she heard emergency sirens she would run to her bed, kneel and pray fervently. She was concerned when she got dressed to make sure things matched. She was crazily energized and yet organized. Kira had just celebrated her third birthday two weeks before her death. Her birthday cards were very important to her and she took them to bed every night, and in the morning she carefully placed them into her doll stroller. When I found them they were in order of importance, ours being first. Her hair was brown with reddish highlights and shone red in the sun, living up to her name. She was a very trusting child, never second-guessing her daddy. I can still see her looking up at him, drinking in every word he said.

I could go on and on but I won't, this description being long already. The hole we feel is so real, but God's grace is real also. The way Kira lived is the way I want to be; do things with my whole heart, be full of joy, without distractions, and fully trusting my heavenly Father. Ironically, Anna's name means grace, and she is definitely living up to it. She has already taken over cleaning out the dishwasher and actually helps! God's grace seems real again to us through her.

On the humorous side we were in the ER again this week. There is a little girl in this house who just sits around fiddling with things. This little girl is not used to having time to herself. Tuesday night Marlea got a little ball from glue dots stuck in her ear. We tried everything but could not get it out. We were just ready to try water and rinse it out when we discovered it was a glue ball, and sticks after contact with water. So in we went again. She thought it was really nice at first to see where Kira was taken and where Daddy had been. She liked all the nurses and the doctor and came home happy, secure, and tired around 12:30a.m. We just couldn't believe that we had to go there again! Maybe she needed to see it and God knew we would never take her there? You just have to wonder what He had in mind!

CLOTTING

After a wound occurs body cells band together and fight, changing so that they effectively eliminate infection and other substances to which they were not previously exposed. The blood helps wash out dirt and germs that may be present from surgery. However, the bleeding soon stops because the blood thickens and clots.

I am changing. The stresses of grief, trauma, and pain are destroying my body makeup. The tears of grief are cleansing my heart of dirt and germs, taking me places that I have not trodden before. Fear, broken dreams, and memories of yesterday seem to haunt my grieving spirit. Simply claiming the grace of God for each day helps stem the flow of tears and in turn creates a longing for God. The clots also help ward off hurts that would normally have felt okay some time ago. After all, I am not who I was yesterday or four months ago. I have changed.

CHAPTER SIX

Jesus through the eyes of a child

At that time the disciples came to Jesus and said, "Who then is greatest in the kingdom of heaven?" And He called a child to Himself and set him before them, and said, "Truly I say to you, unless you are converted and become like children, you will not enter the kingdom of heaven. "Whoever then humbles himself as this child, he is the greatest in the kingdom of heaven. "And whoever receives one such child in My name receives Me; but whoever causes one of these little ones who believe in Me to stumble, it would be better for him to have a heavy millstone hung around his neck, and to be drowned in the depth of the sea.
Matthew 18:1-6

We say we can't see God, and that we trust without sight. We talk about the faith of a child, and read in the Bible that our faith should be like that of a child. The Bible talks about children coming to Jesus in absolute trust. The Bible doesn't talk about children dying. Do they just go Home with Jesus when they die? In my mother heart I fear that she is

33

lonely for us, her parents, and for her sisters. How can a little girl suddenly depart, live without the humans she loved the most, and six weeks later still be happy?

When she was here, did she long for Jesus? When she was conceived and born, did I feel like a stranger to her? As an adult, I asked Jesus to come into my heart. Before a child's innocence is gone is Jesus just there, real and touchable? How good it must feel to a child to be treated with Jesus' love. No wonder a child gets hurt so easily, is so vulnerable, and says things we think are funny. A lot of things that take us hours to process take them only a moment; they are so clear and real to them. Is that because Jesus is a part of them? Can we see God more by listening to children?

Here are some of my experiences from this week:

> Wednesday afternoon I was very sad. I cried and cried. Marlea was angry because she didn't have any playmate. I thought maybe doing something normal would be helpful; so I started sewing and Marlea sat beside me threading buttons, playing with playdough, all things her and Kira used to do together.

This is from Marlea's perspective:

> Mommy was so sad again, with big tears falling down like raindrops. Her tears keep getting in my hair. I wish she would stop crying. I ask, "Mommy, why are you crying?" "Because I am so sad about Kira," she says. I stop a bit and remember last night. Maybe I should tell Mommy about it. "Mommy, last night Kira came down from heaven again and slept with me. Her wings were too big to get into bed so she hung them on the hook where her pajamas used to be. She cuddled up beside me like she always did. Her wings are white and she had a pink robe on again. Mommy, I miss Kira, but I am glad Jesus sends her to me at night.

Mommy, I had more dreams too." My mommy looks down at me hopefully. Feeling the urge to talk I go on. "A while ago I saw Jesus. He was so full of... Glory! He told me to tell my mommy not to be sad." My mommy stops and stares at me. "He said that Kira is going to come back." Then I get a funny look on my face and say, "I think Kira is going to come out of the grave." Maybe if I say something a little funny, she will believe the Jesus part because I know she is supposed to. My mommy cries even more, but now she looks happy. Jesus tells me that I need to help my mommy trust Him more and now I feel so happy because I finally gave her that message. Maybe now she will be happy and be able to understand that Kira is just in heaven. That's really not that far away, and I would like to go there to play with Kira.

From Mom again:

Here is me, God. Here I was so worried about Marlea. Instead I am realizing that You are taking care of me through her. Her sweet understanding in the face of pain and death is so plain and simple. To realize that You even take care of her at night is a great relief to me. On the outside as I gaze at her night after night it doesn't look like that. She is often half sitting up in bed, very unrelaxed. Sometimes it seems as though she is crying in her sleep. To know she is dreaming good things is nice. During the day she is radical, unpredictable, irrational, and insecure, battered by flashbacks just like Merlin and I. Yet she is comforting me. I fully realize how difficult it must be for her to watch me acting irrationally and unpredictably. But to hide from her and to try to hide my tears seems wrong. How will she know how to grieve if I don't allow her to watch me? This vision she had speaks to my soul...it comforts me unlike anything I have experienced yet in this journey. It enables me to trust more, to believe more in Your grace for this grief and life's journey.

On Friday after a rainstorm, half a rainbow was visible, with our house under the middle of the arch. I was amazed. I always heard of rainbows happening to other people but never experienced my own personal one. Different people saw it and said too that our house was in the middle. It's our own promise from God to always care for us even in traumatic situations and feelings.

Our God, Who is big enough to take care of broken little hearts and broken big hearts. God, who loves and knows us, His children. God, who cries with me and sends me touches of heaven through the people and things around us, especially as was shown this week through loving support. God, who gave a message to a brokenhearted child for her grieving mother. I want to learn to trust again, to be able to believe again that He has my good in His hands.

CHAPTER SEVEN

reality staring us in the face

Reality is a summary of real things and events.

Reality is a part of our lives. The gift of shock is leaving and true life is setting in. Reality is my companion all day. Reality lets me sleep, but wakes me in the morning with the feeling of a brick hitting my stomach. During the day I meet it around the corner; sometimes it stares at me from an empty car seat, or the absence of a little girl to put into the grocery cart. It knocks on my heart as I glance at an unused coat hanging by the door; shoes untouched that should be on someone's feet. It seems as though its mission in life is to openly remind me that life will never be the same. Reality waits for me each night in the girls' bedroom as I put two girls to sleep instead of three. My heart does not appreciate this reality; my brain revolts in its presence. My entire being is weary from the clenched fists, tired heart, and the unending knots woven around my stomach.

Sunday's reality seems to greet me in an extra "special" way. Sunday is supposed to be a nice day when one can rest from life's burdens and relax; a day when families are meant to be together and enjoy each other. Reality seems to think it's a nice day for pain to be present in extra measures or to give double reminders. Today it visited me in the form of hearing a three-year-old girl spot her daddy in church. She said, "There's da-da." I turned around expecting to see Kira but alas, I was met with a dose of reality medicine instead. Reality met me after church as I visited Kira's grave; the stark, ugly reality of her lifeless shell, the one that I loved and cherished, being six feet under, and untouchable with my mother hands.

Tonight it greeted me as I ate cinnamon rolls that had been in the freezer, the last ones I made while Kira was here. She loved to roll out her own little portion, and of course eat it later. I grimaced as I chewed down my last bite…wishing that I could bite the reality down with it and never face it again. It hurt as it descended into my stomach. The last time I will ever eat something that Kira helped me make. No amount of brown sugar could have made this cinnamon roll sweet to me. The reality of its symbol is too painful to be covered.

Sometimes reality looks like a sock that fit her foot. A sock she had wistfully picked out at Bass Outlet last winter with crazy penguins hugging all over it. She loved those socks and wore them whenever she could. Now they sit in her drawer, unused. I also like them but the reality of no one ever wanting to wear them again is too much for me to bear. Even if anyone would ever wear them again, the socks wouldn't look the same. They would just look like socks to me; not something crazy that makes me laugh. Reality even seems to have stolen the humor out of the socks. Sometimes when I see a tiny clip that kept many fine hairs off her face, I grab it and stick it in my own hair, wanting to take something with me that belonged to Kira. But even the reality of me needing to wear it in my hair just to feel close to her is too much for me to grasp fully. Reality throws rocks at my heart when I hear Marlea say "Daddy, hold me" favorite words of the one I miss.

Last night reality was my companion as I rocked Anna. Reality met me in memories of rocking Kira to sleep singing her favorite, "Swing Low, Sweet Chariot" softly at bedtime. Reality now is that I will never again be able to sing it without its new meaning. Now to me reality is that Jesus came in His chariot for her. She gladly jumped in and is gone forever from me here on earth. It's not supposed to actually happen to a child…we just like to sing about it. Fear of its reality happening again has replaced the song's gentle lyrics to me. Reality has banished the song from our bedtime rituals. The pleasure has been robbed from the song and is too real for this human body to squeak out any longer.

Reality has not been kind to me in the last week and probably will not be for a while. Sometimes it comes in the form of scenes painted in memory that are full of the awfulness of seeing my child slipping away in front of me with what anyone would think were flu-like symptoms. Time will heal the memories, but never the stark terror and reality of the experience. It is forever etched into my mind.

I want to run, but if I would the reality would be there too. I cry, I pray, I trust, but reality is still here. And so, I stare at it head-on. I dare it to destroy me, to fill my life with pain forever. I dare it to kill my desire to live. I dare it to make me dwell in the past for the next fifty years. I dare it to dash the moment that is called now. I dare it to destroy my ability to enjoy my living children. I dare it to manipulate our marriage with different angles, or turn the memories inside of me into nightmares. Reality seems to fight back at me with all its strength but I don't care.

When I am finished daring it, I embrace it because it is real; because therein I find a peace that only my Heavenly Father can give me. There is no one else to quell the raging storm inside of me; no one else who will walk beside me as I embrace it but refuse the side effects. To feel this reality means that I am still real and will someday experience an inexplicable calmness. Peace that will help me live out of who He wants me to be, and not who I or others think I should be. A peace that comes from knowing that it will be okay eventually, because God can bring beauty out of ashes and rags. A peace that comes from experiencing His grace in a tangible way. Because of the amounts of grace we have experienced, we are convinced that God's other attributes are awesome as well: mercy, truth, faithfulness, love, peace. They must be flowing in abundance! To claim them as part of our lives means we are not able to live on our own… we need God; we are small and needy.

Merlin's birthday tomorrow is another first for us without Kira, but still his birthday. The girls usually helped me make the cake and we made a party out of it. Tomorrow will involve only Marlea and I but we will have fun anyway. The last cake we decorated was Kira's, and we really enjoyed it!

A few months ago I asked Kira how she knows I love her. She replied without hesitation, "Because you give me kisses." I had asked Marlea the same question at the same age and her reply had been "Because you read me books." Love the children God has entrusted into your care. Give them kisses if that is what they want. Exemplify Jesus' love to your children…I wish to, but He holds mine tonight. Every night I whisper in my tears "Jesus, please go get Kira and give her kisses for me." I believe that He does.

free, the way we are made to live

And you will know the truth, and the truth will make you free. **John 8:38**

God created the world to be free. Free to experience life in perfection. Free to dance, run, and dream. Free from pain, turmoil, and failure. Free to reach out and touch a lion, pet a tiger, or chase a bear. Free to run and never tire. Free from the imaginations and terrors of a roaming mind. Freedom from distractions that now plague us. Ultimately, to be free from death and sickness. We were created to be joyful creatures, but also free to make our own choices.

Because of man's free choice we now experience things like death and sickness. Man's freedom was gone forever with one wrong choice. And in its place is only a longing to be free and wild. Oh to run and never have to return to any care! To never have another worry and always experience perfection and joy to the utmost with no effort. In that moment following her choice, the first woman experienced for the first time something all women strongly dislike: change. We hate it, try to avert it, go under it, over it, but change always comes back; and we hesitantly adjust to it many times because we have no other choice. Even after we adjust we often spend lots of time thinking of how it used to be, how nice it was "back then." We tend to miss the moment called now and dwell in the past or future. When we get to the future we are already thinking of the next moment or of the moment that was. It's part of the curse with which we are left because of that bad choice.

Out of that curse, God comes to our rescue with the atoning death of His Son. Once again man can experience freedom and life everlasting. Never changing, Jesus is always the same. He always beckons us to come no matter how ugly we feel, how righteous we might think we are, how lost we become until we get there. He even goes as far as to blot out our sins forever with His blood, if we believe in Him. Through Him we can attain the ability to enjoy the "now" fully. Yes, even when it is painful. He brings the safety and security a woman so deeply desires.

Today in my life I feel this verse *"And you will know the truth, and the truth shall make you free"* —John 8:38. I always thought this verse meant the Bible, which I know it still does. But, today I realize that I know the truth. The truth is that Kira died, that I am left only with memories, some good and some horrific. The truth also is that God has cared for me so well, and that He is taking care of her in heaven. He is and has been so real to me, He has brought truth to me, He has worked through the people around me, and He showed me Himself without me dying. I know the truth… in that I will find freedom. I will not be forever like this; I know the truth… the truth sets me free. I embrace what happened, but I know the truth… Kira was a gift. I even trust God to bless us. I know the truth… He has blessed, is blessing, and will bless us in the future. It might not always be in the way we want it to be, but His grace will be there then as well.

In this I remember the prayer I prayed aloud over and over, sobbing by Kira's bedside, "God I want her to be happy. She was too joyful and free to suffer. God, if she would be happier in heaven, please take her there. I love her too much to watch her suffer here. But, God if she will be okay and happy here, please heal her." God answered my prayer….

The struggle is great. Satan would have us to not embrace the truth. He does not want us to experience freedom. He tries to make life seem as if it will never be joyful again, that we will live with a cloud, and that the cloud will follow us wherever we go. He wants us to believe that God will not ever bless us in any way. He wants us to be too scared to trust in a loving and faithful God. But, God always wins because Satan can't offer freedom! His way is full of lies and bondage, not freedom and truth. The more we embrace the truth, and speak the truth aloud, the more Satan flees. Ironically, the more we speak the truth, the more our hearts believe it as well. This hedge of truth around us will be rebuilt and we will be strong again and able to resist the wiles of the devil. We will again stand therefore, having our loins gird about with truth, the breastplate of righteousness, and the sword of the spirit. In the meanwhile we need people to stand with us, to intercede for us. Thereby we will fight and grow strong again.

Today I think of Kira's way of declaring me to be "in jail" as I have referred to earlier. "Mommy in jail, WHOLE house jail." Yes, life in the house can be like jail, but a beautiful creation awaits outside and I am so glad spring has come. I smile when I think of that; Kira was so crazy sometimes.

CHAPTER NINE

living with pain

For eight weeks I have endured this misery. It hurts, I hurt, we all hurt

I awake, take a breath, and arise; the pain is still here. At night I take my feet off the floor and into bed, I breathe, and close my eyes; the pain remains. I can't get away from life with pain. Pain has become my companion. I have emotional and physical pain. I watch Merlin experience emotional and physical pain. I watch Marlea in emotional pain. Even little Anna seems to have emotional pain sometimes. Hers is released by screaming at nothing, being abnormally attracted to three-year-olds, and still looking for someone who isn't here. My emotional pain comes in waves a lot of the time. Sometimes it comes from situations, things I find that belonged to Kira, and the extra time that I have from her absence. It is always there, part of my new identity. It feels as if my emotional and physical pain have become one.

My mind flashes back to Kira's graveside. I can feel myself getting out of the car. The ground crunches underneath my feet as I walk slowly over to the freshly dug hole. The chair waiting for me is very cold. I look around; my family and friends are gathered around this hole with Merlin and I. Marlea is with Grandma. I thought I would be okay since I had cried so much already. The sound of the casket lid going shut is still echoing in my mind. I wanted to stop there, to not cry anymore, and to protect myself from more pain. I wanted to shut the lid to my heart and, just like the casket lid, never open it again. I decided I wouldn't cry at the graveside, I was finished. But the tears still rolled in torrents down my frosted cheeks. I felt so blank and bland as the minister spoke from God's word and prayed. Songs about heaven were starting as the thuds of dirt began falling on her casket. Yes, Kira. My daughter whom I had loved and cherished was being covered with brown, cold, ugly dirt. Suddenly a burning pain seared through my side unlike I had ever felt. I grabbed at it but it wouldn't go away. Thud, thud went more dirt and the pain continued. I felt as if I were burying part of myself, which is what was happening. As my child, she was part of me. My tears of love for this child overwhelmed my whole body emotionally and physically. This child's body that I had birthed, nurtured, and loved greater than myself was going back to the earth. The dirt still fell and my pain continued as well.

After what seemed like hours later, I stepped away from the grave. There under the maple tree in the graveyard, God showed me in a very real way that my pain will continue beyond this grave. I can cover the hole, but the wound in my heart will stay open with continuing pain and tears. They will keep me soft and pliable. This grave will appear hard, but as time goes by grass will grow and it will become soft again. Likewise my heart feels cold and hard. Through nurture and tears my heart will soften again. The one comfort I have is that the sting of death is gone through the power of the blood of Jesus. In that my emotional pain will heal. My heart that is sliced open will begin to heal. In its place will be a scar, but with God's help I want it to be a beautiful scar. But even scars hurt. The tissue around them stays tender and soft. I want that… I give my pain to Jesus moment by moment… only He who has taken the sting of death away will take the sting of my pain away. Only through embracing this pain will I be able to live joyfully and fully again. Only by walking through this valley will I have the strength to climb and experience the joy of the mountaintop. To go around this will only bring more pain to me and those around me. The pain will stay; it will never be totally gone, but it will not feel so bitter. I again embrace it because out of that desire I will stay real and alive.

The body pain has become part of my life forever. It is not something that will go away, because God created me to want to love and nurture Kira, and I can't. My empty arms feel the pain of Kira never jumping into them again. No other child will ever feel exactly like her and will not be her. I can enjoy other children Kira's age but they are not mine. They don't belong to me, and are not part of me. I can still feel how Kira felt, but it is an unfulfilled ache, a pain that will never leave me completely. It torments my heart and tightens my muscles. To learn to live with pain is an act that I desire to do joyfully and fully.

In some ways the change of seasons brings so many memories and we live the pain of losing Kira all over again. I can hardly bear to watch Marlea play silently and alone outside. It is so boring! I miss the peals of laughter from mud fights, bike riding, and playing in the playhouse. I miss the little hands helping me plant flowers, bringing me dirt and stones. I miss the little hands that last year snipped off all my daffodils and tulips. Flowers were meant for mommies, not in the flowerbed. As I look ahead to Mother's Day I remember last year. Anna was two weeks old when we took her to church for the first time. Now only two little girls ride along and we miss the middle one so, so much.

Marlea wanted to blow bubbles last week so I went outside to find some for her. I found a gigantic yellow bottle that Mr. and Mrs. Bob Lee had given us last year. I was delighted, thinking Mia would have lots of bubbles to blow. I opened it and was ready to pour some into another container. Suddenly I realized the bottle was filled with mud and water instead. I laughed, remembering my little sweetheart and her love for the dirt and water; and also her passion of dumping bubbles instead of blowing them. I guess blowing took too long, dumping is much more efficient. I also cried... missing her.

CHAPTER TEN

to kira

Life Is A Gift
In the beginning God breathed
Life into the human race.
Then death and sorrow, but with hope
Hope of Life—everlasting Life,
In Christ Life is victorious over death
Life for each morning, each moment

It's a Gift.

Life for Kira... she had three years of vibrant Life, close to her Momma being a helper, going with dad-da or kissing good bye, playing with sisters, pushing stroller, learning to ride bike, coming to Ma-maw's house, playing with cousins and singing on the big rock. Going to S.S. class, sitting with Grandpa and much more...

Life was a Gift.

And then death… Kira's lifeless, beautiful, form lay in that crafted treasure chest and on that final day we looked and longed, sorrowed and sang, preached and prayed, and even beckoned our friends to view and weep with us. Then those who held her dearest wept over her once more, rescued a few locks of her lovely hair, and with kind hands and broken hearts closed the lid. Yes, this is final; we drive to the gravesite, put that chest with its earthy treasure into the ground. How painful…how could this be? Many loving hands cover it with sod as children look on in awe with Hershey kisses and daisies to adorn the site… Sorrow, utterly deep sorrow.

But wait; there's Life. Life is victorious over death.

Jesus died, but rose in New Life and even so can we.

It's a Gift.

Kira lives; she is in vibrant Life shining bright by Jesus' side, running in the meadows picking daisies, playing by the brook, singing on the big rocks.

Everlasting Life—it's a Gift.

But now, what about us here; is there Life in the midst of all this sorrow and sickness, loss and loneliness, trials and tears, confusion and cares??

God breathe on us Life…
Life and wellness, joy in sadness,
Strength to continue our journey here
Life for each morning, each moment,

Life is a Gift.

Lovingly written by Kira's Ma-maw, Rachel Glick

Kira, today is the day after Mother's Day. I missed you terribly yesterday and yet in some ways I almost felt as if you were here with us. What all happens that we can't see? Who knows, will we ever know? And when we get to heaven, will we care?

I remember so well last Mother's Day how you were so excited about taking Anna to church for the first time. I was looking at the pictures we have of last year and you were happily holding your baby sister, and so proud. I wish it were last year and everything would be okay. Marlea said today, "I wish we could be a happy family again." But it's not last year. We had a pretty good day. We went to the Make-a-Wish Parade and in the evening some family came over. It was different and somewhat nice.

Even so, nothing could take away the hole that you have left. Nobody can fill the void; nothing can replace you. When I was outside planting flowers I felt like stuffing dirt in the hole in my heart. I tried, but it fell through the cracks. When I am folding towels, I think maybe I could stuff a towel in the hole, but alas, the hole is just as large. I am tempted to fill the hole with food, but I would never fill up. I am tempted to make my life so busy that I don't think about the hole; but it quietly greets me at bedtime. I

laugh at Anna and Marlea, but they can't replace you. No other person will ever be just like you.

I know yesterday you would have come and put your arms around me and said so sweetly, "Mommy, thanks for taking care of me." And that is all; you would have meant it with all your heart. My empty heart tries to feel you, but it's not real because you aren't here to touch, hear, and see. Some days I think maybe washing your dress would be helpful, but I would hang it up again and you wouldn't wear it, just like before. Even my imagination can't fill the hole that you leave in my heart.

So I turn to Jesus. John 14 says "Let not your heart be troubled (have holes), ye believe in God, believe also in me. In my Father's house are many mansions, if it were not so I would have told you. I go to prepare a place for you. And if I go and prepare a place for you, I will come again and receive you unto myself, that where I am, there you may be also." Think of it, the end of life with holes, Kira! Between now and then I promise to only stuff my heart with Jesus. I know you want me to be happy and full of joy, just like you were.

I got Kira's Little Tykes car out of the shed this week for Anna to ride. It still had dirt in the back from Kira. I looked at it and fingered it, remembering how she loved the dirt enough to eat it, throw it at Marlea, put it in her hair, or turn it into a pond. And as I stood there looking at it, Anna started eating it. Was I surprised? No, I was thinking about trying it myself. It must be good!

CHAPTER ELEVEN

fear

For God has not given us the spirit of fear, but of power, of love, and of a sound mind. **2 Timothy 1:17**

We all fear something. Some of us fear having an accident, an earthquake, a house fire, or another natural disaster. Some of us fear people; their opinions, what they might think of us, what they might do to us. A lot of us fear not being good enough for ourselves, or our child or husband not being good enough in someone else's opinion. Most of us fear change. A lot of mothers fear for their child's safety, whether the child is an infant, toddler, adolescent, teenager, etc.

My worst fear was that something would happen to my children. I was always more afraid of something happening to Kira since she was so unpredictable. In plain reality, that fear materialized in front of me. Even now, I can feel the terror of realizing she lost her breath; of picking her up and yelling at her; of hoping she was just having a seizure. I look back and see the events unfolding, and yet in the moment they were so subtle that many mothers would have missed them. What's even worse is had I known, the same outcome would have possibly resulted. The next thought feels full of fear, scary; what if it would happen again, would I know the second time?

I look back again as thoughts roll through my head like a roller coaster. I feel the terror of realizing I need to do something. I feel the terror of yelling at Marlea to get the phone, calling the operator and asking her to help me remember CPR. My heart feels the terror of knowing that my child is the one I have to breathe into, something I always hoped I would never have to do. I feel the terror of realizing she is dying before me and I am alone. I cry to God to save my sweet little girl. My heart feels the relief of hearing my neighbors come inside, who I was praying would come when they heard the call. The fear in my heart is overwhelming by now and I am nearly losing my sanity, but I keep helping, wanting to touch and help my child. My terror only multiplies as the ambulance comes and whisks her off to the hospital. I run outside behind them, watching them throwing their bags in the back. Merlin hastily kisses me and jumps in the front. I go back into the house and scream in fear. More fear than I have ever known in my life. "God, please do something. I can't do this…" I cried out to Him aloud, screaming, yelling, thrashing.

That was only the start of my fear. Slowly I began to realize that God is here with me. My fear culminated on February 24th, when we made the heart-wrenching decision to let her die peacefully… decisions I feared. Fear seemed to consume me as the end came. God calmed my fear with His presence. He let me feel His presence in a real way. When there was nothing left in me, way down at the bottom, God was there.

I will never again say there is something I can't do; nothing seems hard anymore. Even my fear of death is gone forever. Suddenly I find myself with nothing to fear. If God cared for me in my worst fear, He will care for me in all my other worries. I still encounter them, but they flee when I remind myself of God's care in my deepest agony. I picture it as a balloon filled with fear and only a little space left for God tied in the knot. What if I could learn to fill the balloon with God and leave the fear tied in the knot? 2 Timothy 1:17 "For God has not given us the spirit of fear, but of power, and of love, and of a sound mind." Funny that the sound mind is placed at the end after the words "power" and "love."

Merlin reminded me of Kira's favorite song when she rode in the truck with him "Everything's Gonna Be Alright in Christ." She always joined in for the "in Christ" part, pronouncing it "in Tice." I think of that as I go through the days. It's so true.

Life goes on for us. Marlea keeps changing, and definitely healing. I see more and more of the former Marlea coming back. It's wonderful and also helps me feel more normal. Anna is practicing walking and I so much wish Kira would be here to help her. I can just see her taking her hand and walking with her.

CHAPTER TWELVE

how it
used to be

"We have this moment to hold in our hands and to touch as it sifts through our fingers like sand"…

Happy shrieks of laughter, horrific arguments, Anna yelling from being tormented. A sweet little girl finding her momma in the inn kitchen in the morning, calling her daddy on his phone for breakfast, wanting to be rocked all by herself while the others were still sleeping. Two little girls clamoring for Daddy's attention, two little girls running out the door to go with Daddy on a delivery ride, two little girls riding a dirt-bike with their Daddy.

The sounds of four little feet running through the house, two little girls eating supper, two little girls getting a bath, two little girls planning to wear look alike pj's, two little girls listening to stories. One little girl falling asleep during prayer, relaxed in her daddy's arms (at least quite a few nights). Her older sister takes a long time to fall asleep, but Kira is slumbering deeply. Two little girls lying in bed fast asleep, the shrieks of laughter turned into dreamy thoughts and the horrific arguments forgotten. A momma and daddy tiptoe in when weary eyes are closed, smile thankfully, and turn off the light. Now, if we can just convince the baby to sleep, peace will come for a few hours. Later mom and dad come back again and smile, seeing three little girls sleeping blissfully.

These are scenes of the past for us, scenes we enjoyed and loved. Times we treasure, and moments we lived that will never be the same. Reality reminds us they are only memories left entrenched in our minds as pictures, never to happen again in the same way.

In yesterday's place is today.

Instead, one five-year-old feels lost and lonely. One little girl playing by herself, occasional shrieks of laughter from a five-year-old and a baby trying to play together, but few arguments to solve. One little girl eating at the table with two brokenhearted adults all trying to pretend the food tastes good. One little girl riding bike by herself with a forlorn look on her face. One little girl going out the door with Daddy only when greatly persuaded to do so. One little girl to which we read stories and pray, and try to persuade to go to sleep in her big empty bed. Momma and daddy tiptoe in to turn off the light and eye one little girl in bed and a baby in the crib. Later, they tiptoe in again and smile thanking God for two precious little girls, but dreadfully missing the third.

We again cry out to God in our pain desperately needing His grace to sleep another night, live another day. Inside we feel like knocking on Heaven's gate, asking for answers that we can't find here. In our frailty we remember that when we do get to heaven's gate, the questions of this pain-filled earth won't matter anymore. What will matter is that we lived the way God called us to live, with our whole hearts.

Marlea's cousin spent a night and day here last week. When she left, Marlea and I just cried and cried. It was just a touch of how it used to be. And then she left. The pain was unbearable for both of us. Trying to understand pain is difficult and yet so simple for a five year old. At the table some mornings ago Marlea said, "Mommy, how did Kira sound when she talked to her doll?" We both sat in silence looking at our plates trying to remember. Neither of us could, and the pain was so intense, wanting to remember so badly and yet being unable to do so.

Kira learned to ride bike correctly around two-and-a-half years old. A few days before her death, I took the girls across the road to see the cows. The cows were new additions to contribute to our family's nutrition. For the first time, I let Kira ride her bike over to, and even across the road. She was so happy about it. I can still visualize her on the boardwalk at King's, all dressed up in her winter clothes, trying to keep up with her sister. She was wearing a purple coat and hat, with a few brown streaks of her hair falling out of the hat. Later we went into the pasture to talk to the cows. I had to keep telling her to come back; she had no fear of the four-legged animals. They were still getting used to us and my farming instinct told me to stay back a bit. Not her!

CHAPTER THIRTEEN

expectations of God

Expectation: the prospect of something good to happen.

What is my view of God? Do I put myself on a pedestal expecting God to bless me because of what He allowed in my life? I feel sometimes like I hold Him out at arm's length. "God, if you do this, I will…" Is that actually how my heart feels or is that Satan attempting to distort the fundamental belief that God is good? What makes me expect to receive blessings from God? Who am I, but a little person in the eyes of a big God. Just because God took my little girl I now expect Him to bless me with rich blessings? As if compensation were necessary?

The Bible says that God sees a sparrow fall. If God cares about any sparrow, won't He see and bless me? But, why do I deserve His blessing? Am I waiting, like a dog for a biscuit? What if something "bad" would happen? Would I forsake God because my disappointment would be so great? Am I going to live life waiting for something? Or am I going to love God with no reserve, unconditionally. To love unconditionally means to love with all the heart, no matter what happens. Choices seem to stand in front of me that will affect me for the rest of my life.

In all my wonderings and expectations I choose to love. Love is much more fulfilling, more calming, and a lot less worrisome. The other options take too much energy that frankly I don't have. Just deciding to love unconditionally seems like the easy way out. But after all, if God loved me enough to die for my sins, why shouldn't I love? The other options seem so hard for a specific reason. God's love and loving in return was designed to be easy and be accepted.

The human part of me will continue to question, and Satan will continue to try to distort. I might continue to wait for my biscuit but my God, my heavenly Father, understands. He created me with choice, understands my wanderings, and knows that I will come back to love because He knows my heart.

When Kira was about two and a half years old some would tell her "You're cute." With fiery eyes and an insulted look she would say "No! Ki-ki!" Meaning "cute" is not her name, she is Ki-ki. She did the same thing when people told her she looks like her daddy. "No! Ki-ki!" She was her own person; who ever heard of looking like someone else? She was only Kira. We teased her "Kira, are you cute?" Fire! "No, Kiki!" Her daddy loved that line!

CHAPTER FOURTEEN

who am i?

This child changed me and now she is gone. Who am I now?

Who am I? I am a wife and a mother of three girls. Two live here, and one in heaven. But, really I have not been mothering my second-born for the past twelve weeks. Merlin and I married when I was 23 and he 22. Between 23 and 32 I have changed a lot, and some of my changes have been because of having children. They seem to round out the corners of what appeared more like an "all-together person." Kira especially changed me a lot.

When Kira was born I had a fairly big adjustment. With one child I was able to still do some cleaning and manage to accomplish the office duties fairly well. I could still answer the phone without having guests think I was at daycare.

Now with two girls, I had to make some changes and couldn't manage everything without more help. As Kira grew I hardly knew how to handle her energy. She was also awake a lot at night, so I was tired. I got to the point of not being able to sleep anymore. I sought some advice and direction concerning how to deal with myself. I adapted to her and that worked much better. In doing that, I changed mostly for the better, and learned to live life as it comes instead of thinking I had to have it all figured out. That obviously wasn't working with my unpredictable child. I learned to enjoy her, laugh at her craziness, and even join in.

In that, I felt myself revert somewhat to my own childhood. I had been more crazy and carefree as a child. In accepting Kira and enjoying her brought me to more acceptance of myself. I was fifth-born in my family with three older sisters, one older brother, and one younger brother. When I was growing up in my teenage years, my siblings were my examples. They were good examples for me, but I lost myself somewhere in the process. Maybe Kira reminded me of who I used to be as a child? I liked it and felt more like myself and okay with who God made me to be. I felt sometimes like she was leading me; ironically I was the one who had to adapt to survive.

Now that she is no longer here with us I find myself wondering who I really am. How can I still be that person without her? I still want to be the other person with no sadness, no heartaches, and be carefree. Yes, I had bad things happen to me before, but had still lived a fairly sheltered life. I never had anyone die that was really close to me besides my grandparents. They were supposed to die before me.

I had learned to not plan tomorrow, because tomorrow would plan itself. With three children and a bed & breakfast to operate, planning more than one day or one week ahead took too much energy. I never liked date books anyway! I enjoyed being busy with three little ones. I enjoyed watching them relate to each other, play together, and develop their personalities.

Now I can still laugh, but under it I feel a lump and so much sadness that my heart wants to die. I feel like my heart will hurt forever. My carefree attitude seems gone like a vapor, just like Kira. I think of tomorrow and think "Oh no, I will feel the pain tomorrow just like I do today, maybe even more strongly."

Two of my friends came and sent me out for the day. They babysat, washed the sheets, cleaned my apartment, and gave Merlin and I money for lunch. I was happy to get out and think about life. Merlin and I spent time talking about things we had not discussed yet, that had occurred to each of us those five days on the run when Kira was in the hospital. I had time to myself to meditate and think. Mostly, just time to cry. The solitude sent me over the edge. On normal days I can make myself busy or just immerse myself in forgetting what happened and all the pain that is real to me. I am caught in the quietness and calming atmosphere of a different place. Really, who am I? I thought I figured it out and then returned to this messed up home. The people in this home are not acting like they did before. This home seems strange and confusing. Where is the real me? Did she just disappear? How will these things become incorporated into who I am? Maybe it is not something I can control. I feel confused and disoriented, and revert back to the same question. Who am I?

What do I do with all these lessons life has taught me? They are shaping my life whether or not I like it. Do I let them, or do I rebel and run? Can I possibly combine and balance who I am becoming and who I was? But I don't like this new person; I don't want to be her; I don't want anything to do with her. It's not my choice, not my life, not my day tomorrow. God doesn't mind being patient with me. He will bring beauty out of what seems to be ashes to me. And so I relax in the arms of my heavenly Father. It seems so easy; yet is so very, very hard. The amount of pain and confusion that go with it are beyond words.

I feel like the Israelites in the Bible who wandered around in the wilderness for forty years looking for the Promised Land. They had the tabernacle of God with them for direction, and God guided them and has given His Word and spirit to guide me also. My Bible is full of promises and guidance. It contains direction to guide me to Jesus and healing for my confusion and pain. A light traveled with the Tabernacle for the children of Israel. It guided them by day and by night. Today the light of Jesus guides me continually. It has not left me and through following that light I will find freedom from this desert just as the Israelites found their freedom in the Promised Land.

Last night at supper, Merlin threatened to eat all the rest of the ice cream. All of a sudden I could hear Kira saying, "Mia (her name for Marlea), Ki-ki eat whole thing!" Marlea would scream in terror and anger, and Kira would be delighted, with her mission accomplished. I don't remember what all she threatened to eat, but I am sure it was something Marlea really liked! I can still see the look of delight on Kira's face.

broken dreams

Dreams that are no longer mine; mine are broken, lying in ruins at the foot of the cross, waiting for Jesus to heal them.

Last night I dreamed again that Kira was in the hospital, and we were so upset. Everything was so real. The smells, the elevator, even the hallways. I saw her lying there in the hospital bed so still and lifeless with machines beeping all around her. I could feel the tension in my sleep and the desire for her recovery. Then miraculously she recovered. We were so happy to have her home again and enjoyed her so much.

I awoke with a start, thinking it was true and everything was okay again. Disappointment and anger came as I blinked, remembering that no; Kira is in heaven, not back in her bed. Tears rolled in my heart as I tossed in my bed trying to come to grips with reality and be okay with it. God, why? Why is she gone? Why can't I still have her? Why did our dreams for her have to be shattered? Thinking of the dream throughout the day reminded me of our dreams for her....

Kira was so sweet; we had dreams that she would become a lady that brings tenderness and care to people. Kira was joyful; we envisioned her filling those around her with God's joy. Kira was full of energy; we thought of all she would be able to do. Kira was smart; we watched that look of understanding growing in her eyes and realized she could become very intelligent. Kira was beautiful; we dreamed of her being a beautiful woman. Kira was tall; we pictured her at six feet tall, and maybe even more when she would be finished growing.

As I thought of these things I realized the pain of not being a part of these dreams. The dreams I had in my heart of being her mother, helping her through life, watching her discover things for herself, being there for her when the world crashes in, leading her to Jesus, and directing her energy in the right way. Dreams, broken dreams, shattered in several days by just a few fateful twists of events. Those dreams that are no longer earthly dreams; they have turned into dreams of arriving in heaven and seeing her again. Dreams that lay broken waiting for Jesus to heal them and having Him turn them into something beautiful.

One day last fall Marlea and Kira decided that since Daddy didn't do the trimming, they would. They loaded their wagon with the hand trimming shears, broom, hoe (who knows why), and rakes, and wheeled the wagon to the sign on the other side of the fence to do Daddy's trimming. Obviously, they were very proud of it. Kira gave me this cheesy pose. {

the grace of God

Sufficient comfort to embrace the reality of today

What is grace, and from where does it come? Hebrews 4:16 "Let us therefore come boldly unto the throne of grace, that we may obtain mercy, and find grace to help in time of need." To me grace feels so close. Daily, sometimes minute-by-minute I ask God for more. Sometimes I feel as if I am being a beggar, and surely He is tired of me. "Here I am again God, it's me again; I need more, please God." I even get demanding and say desperately "Please God, hurry up, I can't do this on my own." There is always more; grace seems to be in endless supply. **Grace is more about me reaching out and claiming it as my own from God than it is about exhausting the storehouse.**

I am fascinated by what happens when I plead and ask for grace. In asking, I admit that I can't live life on my own; life is too big, beyond my limits. By admitting that I can't do it on my own, I am blessed with an abundance of peace. In feeling peace, I am freed from the cares of life. Sometimes the peace lasts for several days, sometimes for just a minute. Some people go through something hard and look back and say "Had it not been for the grace of God I wouldn't have survived." Presently, I feel God's grace so keenly that I feel it right now. I don't feel as if I could live another minute without it. I am in awe of a God who has an endless supply of grace. I bow in thankfulness, realizing that if it wouldn't be for His grace, I wouldn't have the promise of eternal life. I want to more fully understand the verse in Ephesians 2:8 and live it out for the rest of my life in a deeper way "For by grace ye are saved, not of yourselves; it is the gift of God."

I spread my arms in praise, realizing that I wouldn't have been able to live the horrors of the last months without God's promise of endless grace. I face tomorrow knowing that once again I will be helpless, bent in pain, until I am able to claim enough grace to live that day.

At bedtime Kira would ask Merlin to "sing a new one." He would try, and every time it wouldn't be the right one. Finally, he would sing "Jesus Loves Me" and then she was satisfied. "Jesus Loves Me" was her new song every day! Oh, the simplicity of salvation when it is viewed through the eyes of a child and Jesus' love.

It was hard to celebrate Father's Day yesterday. I feel as if I almost avoided the pain, which may have been good, and maybe not. The pain of not having Kira here with us and of not being able to watch Merlin with the three little girls was enormous for both of us. Our thoughts go back to last year, but it will never be the same; yesterday is gone.

SCAB

The clots keep out harmful bacteria and soon form a scab. The scab acts as protection from infection while the wound is healing. This scab is not usually nice to look at. Most of us tend to pick at it trying to hurry its process. My mother always told me "No, no, don't do that or you will get an ugly scar. It is nature's band aid while the wound heals."

This wound on my heart is beginning to form a scab. This scab will protect me from the normal scrapes of life. It is demanding me to take the time to feel the hurt, the pain, the loss. These feel ugly right now and I would like to pick at them, trying to get them to leave. But without them and their emotions I will not have a beautiful scar. The time this takes causes me to feel disconnected to those around me. They are not doing and feeling what I am. They can try, and that means a lot to my broken heart. But the pain, the grief, and finding God in the midst of this trauma is important for me to discover. This process takes more patience then I ever dreamed possible. The last four months have felt like forever… as if time were standing still.

sunshine and the cloud

To experience and live with this pain remains a mystery to me.

I feel sunshine again. I see it almost every morning as I stumble outside to get the paper. I see it prodding a flower to be real and beautiful. I see it as I look out the window during the day. I feel it in my step, hear it as I sing while working, and as I speak it to my children. I glance across the street and see our cow whose name ironically is "Sunshine." I taste it as I drink the milk she gives. It feels as if God is encouraging me to be brave and feel the sunshine of life. We teased Kira that she and the cow have the same name. Now, I look back and wonder at God.

I feel sunshine as I tramp through the flowerbeds and step on green grass. I gaze in wonder at the sun and its amazing God-given ability to give life to things that lie dormant and ugly.

Amid the sunshine I feel a cloud that seems to follow me wherever I go. It follows me to the store, on vacation, and to church. It even follows me to bed in the dark. The cloud has sadness in it, along with deep sorrow, pain, and frustration. It contains a wish to live the four months and several days over; the new plan would magically be full of miracles. It holds the unending mystery of how life would be if Kira would be here right now. Sometimes it feels like the cloud holds the rain that comes out of my eyes and runs unashamedly down my face. The cloud frightens me. I have never lived with an overshadowing cloud. The more time that passes by, the more this cloud seems to be staying with me for the rest of my life.

The reality is that somehow I need to learn to be okay with the cloud. Right now it seems impossible, way too far out of my comfort zone. I never liked clouds; I always chased them away somehow or figured them out so I was okay with them. This cloud is so different, because God is in this cloud too. This cloud is somehow a tie to the healing process that I haven't figured out yet. Maybe it's not for me to even figure out. Maybe with God the cloud is chased to the foot of the cross. Maybe it will happen and I won't even realize it. Maybe the sunshine will make it smaller. But for now, I want the cloud. I also want it to be a redeemed cloud....

piggy bank from Grandma Glick . Christmas 2008

Today I was doing some cleaning in the girls' bedroom. As I moved the nightstand that used to be Kira's, something shiny caught my eye.

Tucked in between the mattress and box spring were two quarters. I snickered, remembering all the times she would run off with whatever money she could find. Her piggy bank had an unending appetite. Grandma Glick gave it to her for Christmas. It sometimes got so hungry it would eat all of Marlea's money or the change box pennies. I don't know where the quarters came from that I found today, but something tells me they weren't

disconnected

I am disconnected from this world I live in, connected only to my own whirling spiral of grief.

I feel disconnected. Over four months later I find myself wondering, "Did this really happen to me, am I sure it happened, or is it just a bad dream?" I look outside and see someone walking past on the road or next door; maybe it happened to them and not to me. I see someone at the store; maybe that was their child I heard about. I meet a car on the road; maybe they have an empty car seat. I have trouble remembering who I am or how old I am. I have trouble remembering what the pain is that I am feeling so strongly. I get mixed up and upset about strange things that have no significance in comparison to the real pain that I feel.

Today I wanted to remember someone's name. I couldn't remember, as if that part of my brain had just…evaporated. I knew the person, but the name completely vanished from my memory.

I have trouble identifying the issue when my children are upset; after all, what really are they feeling? How am I to know when their little minds don't understand everything? So I falter, guess, and guess again. Sometimes I am right; sometimes I am way off. Usually they are just like me; confused, searching, and hurting, but expressing it the opposite way. What appears to be a lost shoe can actually end in a discussion about a lost sister. What appears like misbehavior in reality is a hurting little girl wishing for her sister. What I thought was disobedience today ended up to be a fear of picking up toys because of having to do it alone. It's so completely disconcerting even to a child when there is a surface issue, with the real issue somewhere underneath.

Sometimes I need to be reminded that it is summer and not fall or winter. How would I know when I can hardly recognize beauty? Oh, that is right; flowers don't usually bloom in the winter. I forget to water them, thinking rain had come just yesterday, when in reality the rain had come a week ago. I look at a picture of the five of us and wonder who those people were. I wish with all my heart to feel the middle child on that picture and know her now, again, today. I remember the pain, the reality, and the happenings of the last months. Today I remembered it by reading the blog from February 24th. Tears came, and I couldn't deny the truth of reality; it sounded too familiar. I am the mother, we are the family, and Kira was our child/sister. She is gone; my worst nightmare became reality.

I am not the same, and I never will be. I am confused, hurting, wounded, and it's okay. Someday there will be no more pain, sickness, death, sorrow, or crying. I will live today with life in perspective of heaven because there is no other way in which to live. I will live today knowing that God has me in the palm of His hand because there is no other way I can survive. I will live today because I am blessed to still have two little girls for which to care and a husband who loves me. Today I am blessed to have a God who knows me and understands my wanderings, my confusion, and my disconnected feelings.

As I lay in bed tonight putting Marlea to sleep I was reminded of Kira. She was sometimes scary to lie beside in bed, not so much in the last six months as before that; if she was upset at me for some reason, I needed to watch out. She had strong legs and very good aim. Somehow, she always managed to kick me soundly in the stomach. If she didn't aim for my stomach, she went for my face. Her aim was impeccable and produced some kind of fulfillment for her. Her mother, on the other hand, was not at all amused.

wanted: a map

Whether you turn to the right or to the left, your ears will hear a voice behind you, saying, "This is the way; walk in it." **Isaiah 30:21**

Map: drawing showing route or location; a diagrammed drawing of something such as a route or area made to show the location of a place or how to get there.

Today, July 13 is my birthday. On my birthday I like to plan a little about the next year. What will I do, who will I become, what would I like to change to become a better person?

I wish for a map that would tell me where to go in life, and what to do with all my feelings and thoughts. A map that would give me some kind of direction about how my sorrow and pain will become redeemed and beautiful at the foot of the cross. A map to tell me how to let it be redeemed; how to let it become beautiful.

A map to direct which way I should go. Right now I feel as if I am being pulled in all directions. The feelings are interpreted by denial, anger, bargaining, depression, and the most encompassing one, acceptance. The acceptance is also the most confusing because I will never be okay with what happened to Kira. My acceptance has to do with being redeemed by Jesus.

I wish this map would also tell me who I will become after this fight. How do I know what to feel if I can't see the end result? I have no idea who I will become, or who I am even trying to become because I am not trying to become anyone, and yet I am changing. But really what has changed is the direction in which I am going; my goal is heaven more than ever before.

There is a map to heaven; it is the written Word of God. That can be frustrating because I have trouble absorbing what I read, so that brings me back to the beginning, wishing for a map. But alas, there is none to tell me exactly where to go, or what to feel. It is uncharted territory to me. I have never been here before, and I have no experience. No one else does either, since every situation is different. Advice and insight help tremendously, but really in the end it is us, Kira, and what happened. And the power I tend to forget about, the One who will guide me if I just let Him, the One who waits until I ask for direction, is Jesus. I have been thinking about this for weeks already; and since then God brought a major happening into my life that was far beyond anything I imagined would ever happen. The healing I experienced from the incident was really amazing. From this experience I can more easily trust that God is in control. But it takes a tremendous amount of trust and being okay with the "lost" feeling.

Last year on my birthday we went to Chili's restaurant, and took the girls along. We had a great time, but I never got to eat my food; I had to bring it home and eat it later. We were so busy keeping the three girls happy I didn't even mind eating it later. As I remember the keeping happy became a joke; Marlea was fussing, Kira's tummy hurt, and Anna was crying. I wished for it tonight. We were only four tonight and each of us was quite well behaved in comparison. The fifth person might have been acting like a little lady, too? It was almost as if I could reach out and feel her presence. And yet touching her was unattainable, just beyond my reach. The hole....

CHAPTER TWENTY

coincidence

Something that is said to "Just happen"

We say it all the time "coincidence." We believe it as we hear a crazy story. We act as if it were coincidence when we tell something that happened. We walk along the road and just happen to see a friend. We call someone and they just happened to intend to call us. We read a book and just happen to have a need met. We open our Bible and happen to find just the right verse. Do things just happen? Does anything like coincidence exist?

The last four months I have been thinking a lot about the whole ordeal and events since then. The many things that have happened were so "right." When I called 911, an operator answered that met my needs perfectly. She responded with exactly what I needed; she has touched me in ways I didn't expect. She allowed herself to give of her own emotions, entered my world in a way that only she could. She gave more to me than just CPR directions, she gave her own heart. In a matter of three minutes my neighbor was charging into the house; I didn't even know him then. He came complete with EMT training and a bag of medical emergency stuff. In about eight minutes the ambulance was here and soon Kira was in the ambulance. It wasn't coincidence… it was amazing! This was so fast for everything to happen! I know all this because the emergency operator was timing it. In just over twenty minutes Kira was at the hospital.

At Hershey Kira didn't just happen to have the right nurses. They were all so gentle and caring; I firmly believe we had the perfect nurse for each day we were there. They stood beside us and grieved. They allowed themselves to become attached to us even though they knew we would leave again and depart from their lives. Coincidence, no… God! The doctor she had was exactly the right one; the more he learned about her, the more he loved her. He sorrowed and wept right with us. God knew we needed him; it was no coincidence. God also knew I would need the counselor. He gave me words of truth and life at a time in my life when I was desolate. Coincidence that he had the right words to bring me to the cross; no… God!

Since then I could recall countless times when I received cards with exactly the right verses and words from people who care. I could tell of numerous times when my devotional in the evening was exactly what I had been thinking all day. The one night after writing a blog and using a verse, the same verse was in my devotional. Coincidence, no… God! God is so much bigger than we think He is. It is so beyond our comprehension how insignificant we are, how God can be everywhere at one time, and how much He cares for us.

These things I mentioned here are from God. I don't believe in coincidence anymore. There have been too many. I firmly believe that God is the Controller of this universe and every little detail that happens in it. Yes, bad things happen. Bad things happened to me but look how God cared for us in spite of it all. I can't get around it; I honor the God of heaven and earth!

In the morning when I am doing breakfast for my guests I miss Kira very much. She often awoke earlier than the other two. If I had finished making breakfast I would hold her on the rocking chair and rock and cuddle her. I would sit there as long as she wanted. It was her "momma time." Last week I was thinking about it and missing her. What do you know, that morning Anna woke early and has been quite a few mornings since. Coincidence;

no… God! No, she won't replace Kira, but it was a touch of heaven to me. I miss those momma times with Kira… Jesus, please hold Kira for me. Oh, the pain that goes with trusting that Jesus knows how to care for her is beyond describing!

CHAPTER TWENTY-ONE

talking

Step out of your comfort zone today and offer meaningful Jesus words to the people around you.

Talking is an amazing act of the brain, vocal cords, tongue, and mouth. It's what we use to communicate our heart, our feelings. By using this tool we convey to other people who we are. We base our opinions of people a lot by what they say. We use quotes from people who died many years ago. People leave their stamp on life and are remembered by what they say or, don't say.

Sometimes we are not sure what to say, and the wrong words come out at the wrong time. We want other people to share their feelings, but we might have to ask a simple question first. That simple question is the bridge, a bridge into people's hearts. We often say it in casual conversation but really rarely mean that we will spend the next hour listening to how they really are. It has become almost slang to some of us. "How are you" can open a can of worms in some situations. We don't really want to know but feel obligated to ask the question out of politeness.

Picture with me an old concrete bridge, the kind with big round half-circles in the bottom for boats to pass through. There is a break in this bridge. Across the gap lies a skinny two-by-four. Care, love, and concern are on this bridge. But on the skinny two-by-four are your words. They open the way to meaningful conversation, heart feelings, or intense struggle. They might be what that person needs to feel God right at that minute. One can be intensely alone but words can change it all around in minutes. Someone might be hurting but kind words or questions can bring that person out of despair and straight to Jesus. Another might be thinking nobody cares, but your question is "a little bit of Christ" to him or her. We are generally scared to talk seriously, especially in anything involving intense pain. We are scared to ask that simple question.

On the other hand, if asked that question, some are afraid to be honest. Satan loves to make us feel alone, lost, and in despair. Martyr-style feelings work great for Satan. He delights in silence when it involves pain. Jesus wants us to bridge that gap; He calls us to be caring, gently guides us to ask questions, and gives us the strength to relay our feelings to others so they know how to care for us.

Talking also connects happenings in our lives. Situations change us; talking bridges that gap and connects us to the person with which we are communicating. It connects us because we feel care, love, and concern for each other when we talk.

Today two people stand out in my mind when I think about talking. Both of these people wouldn't have had to ask me any questions; they wouldn't have had to share personal experiences with me. But they did; they braved it and looked me in the eye. They cared enough to take the time to encourage me. They were "a little bit of Christ" to me. The one person I met briefly maybe twice. The other I had never met before. In turn, I listened intently to their words, their story. I cared about their pain in a way that I wouldn't have been able to care before. If only I could have been like this without being in such intense pain myself. After our conversations I felt the gap being bridged again in my life. I was "okay" again for a while and could go on with the day.

Others have also bravely bridged this gap for me at different times. They have symbolically held our family's hands and walked that two-by-four with us. They have drawn me in, intentionally including me in conversations. Their ability to attempt to enter my world even though they haven't been able to feel everything has been a huge gift to me. They have braved that "dangerous" two-by-four and kept us connected to others. They have gently encouraged us to talk, to share our feelings and intense struggles.

Jesus did it too. Even on the cross he cared for the sinners being crucified with him. Even in his deepest pain, emotionally and physically, he stayed present in the actual situation. The thief on the cross voiced his need by asking Jesus to "remember Him." In turn Jesus' comforting response to the thief "Today thou shalt be with me in Paradise" was part of the bridge to heaven for him. Without these words he would have died in deep emotional pain and eternity in hell. These words that form our talk are healing balms.

Kira was just becoming a little lady. She was leaving the two-year-old world and entering the world of a three-year-old. Linda, my sister-in-law, shared a memory with me this weekend of the last time she had been with Kira. When we arrived for Christmas, Kira came up shyly beside her and said "Hi." So sweet, so her. I can feel her beside me now saying, "thanks for supper, Mom." I guess God makes the little ones who are more high-maintenance sweet so the good outweighs the bad. They are heart-melters.

the love of God

I pray that Christ will be more and more at home in your hearts as you trust in him. May your roots go down deep into the soil of God's marvelous love. And may you have the power to understand, as all God's people should, how wide, how long, how high, and how deep his love really is. May you experience the love of Christ, though it is so great you will never fully understand it. Then you will be filled with the fullness of life and power that comes from God. Now glory be to God! By his mighty power at work within us, he is able to accomplish infinitely more than we would ever dare to ask or hope. **Ephesians 3:17-20**

I want this. I want to know, experience, and to have Christ at home in my heart. I want deep, long, unmovable roots. I want to understand; yet the Bible says I never will fully comprehend. I want the power, the boldness, and the energy that goes with it. I want the glory of God to emanate from my life in a shining, bright sort of way.

As I repeatedly read this passage I cried and cried. I don't understand the things God has allowed into our lives. But neither do I understand the love God has for me as His child. And His love is so much greater than anything else I know. The small taste I have and know about is that if I can really grasp that God loves me like this, anything that happens in life will be okay; because with love, God has my best in mind. But I am human and so little compared to God. So therefore, will I ever really get it? And yet I read that I will then be filled with the fullness of life and power that comes from God. I choose again to love, to believe, and to trust.

At the mountains this past weekend I was reminded of Kira. One picture in my mind is of Kira out in a huge lawn following her daddy as he played a game. Nothing else mattered except trotting after him. Never mind that other children and playthings were around to enjoy. She wanted to be with Daddy so it didn't matter how long or hard she had to walk. On the flip side, I think of this and am vividly reminded of our loss in her dedicated following. But I enjoy the memory. It is embedded in my mind, and it reminds me of what I want to be like with my heavenly Father....

STRETCHING

Underneath the scab, the skin is healing. New blood cells are being made to repair the wounded skin. Damaged blood vessels are being fixed. The new skin is stretched, itchy and tight. White blood cells, the kind that fight infection to keep a body from getting sick, go to work by attacking any germs that may have gotten into the cut. White blood cells also get rid of any dead blood and skin cells that may still be hanging around the cut. By the time it's all done, a new layer of skin will have been made. Eventually, a scab falls off and reveals new skin underneath.

I am being stretched way out of what is "normal." It feels as if I want to be put back together but have many "feelings" in the way. Not to mention that I am irritable, tight, and just tired all the time. I thought I was at the bottom, only to sink further. My heart is being purged down to the essentials of life. No infection is left, no nothing actually. I need to allow the people around me to love me, care for me, and lift me up in prayer to Jesus, our ultimate healer. Perhaps I need to face my fears, stretching me so that the scab can and will fall off or get "picked off." Perhaps I am not listening to my spirit, soul, and body correctly. Perhaps I need to rest, rest, and rest. Rest my weary heart; find solitude for my soul, and a horizontal position into which my body can collapse. Perhaps that is what would really stretch me, to rest to be still.

"You gain strength, courage, and confidence by every experience in which you really stop to look fear in the face. You must do the thing you think you cannot do." —**Eleanor Roosevelt**

disappointment

Pursuing a ray of hope beyond the valley and just ahead only to be crushed halfway up the next small hill…

Disappointments are faced every day. Today I am disappointed that life isn't turning out like I thought it would. I feel disappointment in my heart from not being able to understand God's whole picture from the beginning of my life. If He would let me see it, I would know and wouldn't be disappointed because I would know what to do and when. Instead, I am dealing with disappointment. My heart feels uncertain what to feel because of the disappointment inside.

I find myself wary to trust God, wondering why God gave choices in life. I can choose to trust, and I can choose to feel disappointment. Why do I think it has to be my way… why do I think this is God's plan B for our lives? What if this is God's plan A? Am I going to be okay with that or am I going to feel disappointment in God for the rest of my life because I think this is plan B? I want what I thought was plan A. I am disappointed that we now have to live in plan B; can I choose to believe that God is sovereign?

I am disappointed because again God has taken life away. A few days ago I lost the baby I had carried for fourteen weeks. We thought this pregnancy was nice, and that a baby would help us to heal. Together we again felt this horrible pain. No one could soften the words from the doctor's mouth as she gently told us that the results of the ultrasound are that there is no life, and has not been for probably five weeks. There were no more words to say; she could have tried to mumble some more, but those words would not have meant anything. We felt utter disbelief as we stared blankly at her; the doctor was very aware of the pain and sorrow we were already experiencing. No words were spoken as we walked numbly to our vehicle. I could feel Merlin entering his no-zone place of too much pain, too much overload.

Over the weekend ahead we were going to share the fun news with my family on vacation. The happiness would be a welcome distraction from the pain of Kira not being there. A weekend earlier we were with Merlin's family and had really felt good sharing about the coming baby. Its birth would have almost been on Kira's birthday. What a nice surprise to go with the pain of not being able to celebrate her life here on February 6th.

Instead the weekend was filled to the brim with pain. Instead of happiness, we cried so much about Kira. Our happiness dashed, we mourned for the death of our unborn child and what the next days and weeks would be like for me physically and for all of us emotionally. Most of the time I felt as if I couldn't even mourn after experiencing such a small loss compared to what I was feeling missing Kira. Some of the time I became overloaded in the jumble of confusion, not sure what to feel, or when. I felt convinced that a nice thing will probably never happen to us again. We will just constantly be bombarded with sorrow upon sorrow.

As the weekend went on I became more and more miserable and wanted to go home. Strangely enough my sister Renita did also. In the end the Lord strongly rebuked me for thinking the nice things always happen to someone else. My sister also lost her baby due to miscarriage. We both ended up in the hospital a day apart. Instead of being alone on this journey God gave me my own sister to walk by my side, and gave her me to walk by her side. I was grateful for her tender loving care and understanding heart. She had already walked this valley of grief so well with me, and to have her understand me in this as well was truly a gift. Also strangely this gift was at her expense. To me it didn't seem right at all. We can't decide who will walk our pain with us or be in similar circumstances. Even more trust in God's sovereign power is required when someone hurts that you love a lot, like your own sister.

The emotional pain was really intense for me, but I had so much physical pain that it masked the emotional pain very well. In some ways it was nice, but in other ways it made me realize that I was already so emotionally drained that it was simply more bags on the pile. The ability to feel seemed gone; this wasn't grief but only disappointment of things not going the way I thought they would. I gave up; my own will was still left to God.

I chose to give up my will and totally trust God's sovereignty. With that decision I felt a peace and the knowledge that life is okay. To believe that God is sovereign creates a strong thread that winds me tightly in my Father's embrace. I picture myself in the Father's arms; not because I have to, but because I want to be there. I feel broken there, yet loved. I feel tears because with that embrace I choose to believe that God knows what is best for me and for our family. My disappointment is replaced with an amazing sense of trust, security, and loyalty toward my heavenly Father.

The pain of a miscarriage is not insignificant. It cannot be masked simply as something that happens and not just merely disappointment. Normally I would have felt a lot more. Emotionally I simply did not have the energy to struggle with God or embark on the grief spiral again; I was already there. All the emotion I could muster was simply disappointment. I was in some ways already experiencing the rest of the emotions. This child was important to me; more importantly, though, was that I accepted God's will and what happened. Sometimes nature has a way of removing what is not normal. I had felt unusually well during those fourteen weeks, so I could more easily accept what happened because of being already suspicious something was wrong. I also felt strongly that God wanted me to learn more of Himself and His sovereignty. If you have experienced a miscarriage and feel a lot more emotion than I did, please do not condemn yourself. God calls us to embrace the times and seasons that He brings us. Sorrow can bring growth and character, though laughter seems more pleasant. Above all, remember that God is sovereign.

Last summer the girls had this hang-up on getting mad at people who came close to our porch. For those of you who don't know us, we live at a bed and breakfast, and our front patio connects onto the parking lot for our guests. One morning last summer Kira was out there with me and along came one of our guests. Kira, without batting an eye said "Hey, old man!" I nearly died of embarrassment. I appreciate this guest and his family very much and felt terrible that my two-year-old daughter would talk like that. I still don't know from where those words came. The worst part of that statement is the consideration that children usually repeat words from their parents; so one could assume that is how we talk when no one is around. That of course not being true, but how could we prove that when our two-year-old pops off a statement of such disgrace? Fortunately for me, my guest was very gracious and understanding! Any amount of graciousness couldn't take away my embarrassment, though!

CHAPTER TWENTY-FOUR

rest

Come unto me all ye that are heavy laden and I will give you rest. Take my yoke upon you and learn from me, for I am gentle and lowly in heart, and you will find rest for your souls. For my yoke is easy and my burden is light.
Matthew 11: 28

Does anything on earth that we can experience now compare to rest? I ponder things; I try to figure out the days ahead, and my mind wanders. That is not rest. I work all day, and when I sit down I think about what I could be doing…that is not rest. I go to a party with my children and husband, and run after children all evening (I wish to have to run more!). That is not rest. On Sunday, I think I will rest. Instead, I care for my family. Although I love it, it is not rest. My heart wants to rest, my mind wants to rest, and my body wants to rest. Rest, is there rest anywhere? Does a mother ever really rest with both eyes shut and her brain turned off? I am exhausted, and I am weak. I feel as if I am making my body work when I would like to rest all day long.

More than that, can my heart rest? Can I be so okay with disappointment, pain, and reality that I feel rest? Can I in my simple human-ness effectively turn my struggles over to Jesus and just rest in Him? The actual reality of trusting in Jesus will bring rest.

My desire to fight is gone. My desire to be me and who I want to be or think I should be is gone. My desire to control my circumstances is gone. What's the point anyway? I have no energy to challenge or question God. Resting in Jesus is so much easier. Rest brings peace, dismisses struggle, lessens stress, and results in a joyful attitude toward life. Rest is way at the bottom of the struggle; it's a giving up of my will.

In its place comes a filling of God like I have never experienced before. I feel no need to get upset with the trivial things of life. I feel in its place a passion to live for God; a passion to encourage those around me; a passion to keep my eyes set on Heaven! I feel more mercy from God than I ever did before. Endless mercy! It makes rest even more peaceful. The ultimate rest is Heaven. But I am amazed at the rest Jesus has to offer me here on this earth. It is just a taste of Heaven! *"Come to Me all who labor and are heavy laden AND I WILL GIVE YOU REST. Take my yoke upon you and learn of me. For I am gently and lowly in heart, AND YOU WILL FIND REST FOR YOUR SOULS. For My yoke is easy and My burden is light"* **Matthew 11:28-30**.

A few months ago Marlea and Kira were playing doll and dress-up. They both had/have imaginary husbands. They both came to me with longing looks on their faces. The words that came out of their mouths astounded me. "We want husbands. You have Daddy, but we don't have husbands." I could hardly keep a straight face. I said something about praying for one for when they are older. I keep that memory tucked into my heart, remembering

that Kira is being loved perfectly by her heavenly Father.

six months

Halfway to a year without someone dear

Six months used to be a long time. In six months, we went from snow and cold to the end of summer. School had three more months to go six months ago, now school starts in only several days. Six months ago we wore coats, gloves, and mittens.

Six months ago I vividly remember walking into Hershey Medical Center. My sister was with me. I was wearing a coat, long socks, and a sweater. I remember feeling the bitterly cold wind since my coat was open. The cold stung my face and swirled inside my coat. I didn't care, cold was so much less painful than what I was feeling in my heart. My heart was full of more pain than I ever knew in my life. A few days earlier my life was happy and full of life. Now I was walking toward this building where my daughter lay lifeless; the sweet little girl who just a few days earlier had been running around after her big sister. I knew as I walked that I would be faced with hard decisions in the next hours, and that I actually wasn't counting on leaving with my daughter. I thought the undertaker would be taking her, not me. The cold seemed to go with the pain I knew would be mine to embrace in the next twenty-four hours.

So I embraced the pain the cold gave me almost willingly. I silently thanked God that at least the weather matched the circumstances in my life. I bowed my head and pressed on toward that door of the hospital, determination driving me on. Determination to be the mother God wants me to be: strong, courageous, and gentle. To be the mother my little girl needed even though she couldn't see or hear me, even though it was only my touch that mattered to her body. That night I pressed on; up the elevator; down the hall to PICU. And to my heart-broken husband. To my ever-faithful family and friends who were with us night and day those five days in the hospital. Most of all, to my little girl who needed me in her last night on this earth. I lay beside her most of the night, heart-broken. I went through the events of the next day with basically no sleep. I watched the last brain tests knowing what the outcome would be. Together, Merlin and I endured the torture of telling Marlea that Kira was going to die. We held our daughter as her heart-wrenching wails reached to heaven and way down the hall.

Memories seem to flood me as I think of the happenings of six months ago. Yes, that hallway and the doors to the forbidden PICU. The smell is still with me. I can feel the number of footsteps necessary to get to the room in the far corner. It had a door on it...bad sign. I notice some of the others don't. I can feel myself in that room... the thoughts and feelings come back and our experiences there in that room at the corner of the building.

There was a window with views of grass and trees in the background. My brain can recall the beeping noises...counting the heart rate of our little girl. I can feel her body on me as we sang lots of songs that last night. First Merlin held her, then I. The songs seemed to go on forever —I wanted them to do so. The longer we sang, the longer I could hold my little girl. One last time. The last time I would hold her here on this earth. Maybe forever? Do people grow in heaven? I don't know. What I know is that when we are finished singing the doctor and nurse will come in and turn off this machine. A few days ago when they did breathing tests they removed the machine and manually breathed for her to see if she could breathe on her own. She didn't. For a long eight minutes she lay there not breathing while Merlin and I watched, full of fear. I knew this time we wouldn't hook the machine back up. It would just be more of what I experienced a few days ago when I did CPR on her for those long ten minutes. That felt like death. This would be death. And yet I knew it was time. Time to let go of her suffering body. Time to stop dreaming that she was going to wake up. Time to accept the reality and limitations to her human body.

Entrenched in my fear I feel Merlin looking at me. He asks "Are you ready?" I bleakly nod. Nothing else to do, nothing else to try, no more hope. It's all dashed and all ending in this. I hear the doctor come in; tears are streaming down his face. We nod. He unplugs the machine. He and the nurse step to the back, heartbroken. They tried, they did their best. They too hate ends like this. Our brothers and sisters and parents are gathered around the bed. Merlin is beside Kira and I, his head bent in sorrow. I see and hear my brother go on his knees, arms and hands uplifted toward heaven pleading with God for mercy. Mercy for me. I start singing "Swing Low, Sweet Chariot." I am still fighting inside of me. Seems so wrong to be singing this song, her bedtime song, and this is really happening. Why did I ever think this was a nice song to sing to her at bedtime? Then I remember; because it relaxed her. So I sing with my heart and tears coming in torrents.

About the first verse I feel it. Something is happening. I know the machine is off because her heart is slowing down to nothing. But the sound? Where is it coming from? My eyes are open but I see nothing here that would make this noise. The sound gets louder and I realize the sound is like chariot wheels whirling in the air. In reality here in this bed this body of Kira is getting light in my arms. I feel mystified; they are whirling away with my little girl inside. I get a glimpse in hindsight of only the wheels. But the sensation has me in a stupor. I can still feel it; it started in her toes. No words can describe it more than a sensation. It continued up through her body as I was singing. First I thought it to be my imagination. By the time it got to her waist I knew I was feeling something heavenly. It was slow and deliberate. I was not here… I was being transported with her.

With my eyes open and still full of tears and my mouth still singing I saw my little girl in heaven. On the shores of a beautiful beach, she and Marlea were playing. She ran away with Marlea chasing her. And the giggles were coming full throttle. Marlea ran after her, shouting for her to come back. Kira kept running toward the light. It was a bright light. Very bright. As she ran it became more apparent to me that the light was the form of a man. Kira hid in the light—still giggling. The light was too bright for me to look upon. I could glance at it, but the face was hidden. There was no guessing; there is only one person that we cannot stand to look upon. Instinctively in my mind I thought of Moses who could not look upon God. But no, I am still here in this bed at Hershey Medical. Did I die?

No, I realize that I can still hear those around me. In fact, I am still singing Swing Low, Sweet Chariot. Kira's body is still lying on me although I know she is gone. Then why could I see her there? My brother is still at the foot of the bed with his arms outstretched toward heaven. Then I felt amazement all over again. All I could say was that Kira was getting lighter and lighter in my arms. I soon got out of the bed and just stood there in a daze. I wanted to go under the bed, out of the room, or anywhere I could get away from the glory. My human body could not bear the overwhelming feelings. The desire to hide persisted and I started to sing again, this time about the blood of Jesus. The blood of Jesus was the only reason I could stand the glory of God. Others said I shone. God's presence in the room was tangible.

My overwhelmed feeling was brought back to earth with a look at my husband. Oh no, he was going to pass out. Over twenty people in a small room seriously deplete oxygen. The white sheet still kept coming... he soon was on the floor. Yes, basically passed out. The nurses took care of him. He was revived after a drink and some fresh air. I guess it got too hot in there. Truth was, he too wanted to die. At that distinct moment I realized that as this journey of pain continues; we will grieve differently. Later as we wheeled him out in a wheelchair he brought us some shreds of humor. We, by God's grace, endured the most horrible pain a parent can endure. We quietly said good-bye to the nurses and doctor, gathered Kira's things, and stumbled out to our vehicle. The ride home was unbearable. We were so tired, heartbroken, and drained. The thought of the four of us coming in the door without Kira was horrible. Physical strength straight from the throne of God was our only sustenance. That, and lots of grace. I don't look back and say, "Wow, I don't know how we did it." There was no other way but God. He was and is so real to us. I still say I don't feel as if we would have been able to physically and emotionally experience God like we did that night without the prayers of caring folks.

Six months, but my mind relives the scenes in the vision every day. Scenes that will stay with me for the rest of my life. This experience has held me through the darkest time of my life. Yes, my Father knows me. He alone knew and knows how hard this journey is for me. He knew I would need tangible evidence of Kira's happiness to keep my heart from breaking. He knew what I would need to help me learn to trust Him again. Above all, my heart has been strengthened in my belief in God. A God that simply knows us and loves us for who we are. Yes, six months have passed since I saw and held my daughter. It is also six months of knowing God like never before. Dark times when the Light was all my heart and mind could see. The Light, the Light, the Light. I am going for that Light. I was afraid of death. Not now. It was nice. The most glorious, peaceful thing that ever occurred in my life. No, saying good-bye to Kira was not nice. But death is not scary for the redeemed.

A few days ago I found Marlea on the floor holding Anna. She was singing a song. "You are my sunshine, my only sunshine, you make me happy when skies are grey, if you only knew Kira how much I love you, please don't take my sunshine away." She looked at me sheepishly and grinned. The pain was radiant on her face. I turned away, wanting to hide my tears, remembering the many times she sang that song to Kira. She wanted to sing it to Anna, but it felt like betrayal to Kira to use Anna's name instead. In a way, it gave me a clear picture of the pain she still faces every day. The pain that comes out in other ways besides words.

I spent the day sewing for my mother; doing something for someone else felt so appropriate. Most of all, I felt God strongly encouraging me to enjoy our children that are still here. I did, and in a way the day became so much fun and bearable. None of their names are Kira, but I saw sunshine on their faces!

the circle

A circle left to itself will continue its patterned cycle

The grieving process seems to be a circle. It goes around and around, and never stops. It pauses briefly at each feeling; sometimes the feeling lasts a week before it continues. The main factors in this circle include denial, anger, bargaining, depression, and acceptance.

They begin to feel like part of my life… and I am not sure that I like it. At first these factors were visitors and I embraced them because it seemed like the hospitable thing to do. But to stay? I didn't invite them to stay, let alone become an ongoing circle. This circle is violent at times and very unkind to my emotions and body. I feel bunchy, on edge, and a bit tipsy. The temptation to just cave in and crash is real. It would be nice to spend weeks in bed totally unaware of the world around me. But something holds me in the circle like a magnet. It calls me gently to be real and gracefully endure the emotional pain with strength that is not my own.

So I decided to talk to God about it last week. God gently, oh, so gently, encouraged me to slide one factor out of the circle and see what happens. Ironically I find myself starting with "denial." This particular visitor can really throw me out of shape. It makes tears come in torrents, and anger come in bushels. I revert and pretend in my mind that it is before February 19. I imagine we are in Ohio, our last trip together. I envision us at the Farm Show weeks before Kira's death. I think of the day before her illness and relive it in my mind simply wishing that we could just skip February 19 on the calendar. I wonder what the next days and months would have been like for us without her sickness and death. Denial pushes reality into the distance as my mind teases me with thoughts of how peaceful life would be. My mind and body can relax for a minute as peaceful thoughts come and I can deny life as it is today.

Reality drags me back to my real life. The life that I feel is crushed and lifeless. Anger sweeps in and takes over like a raging fire. It seems as if someone or something should be to blame. The "what ifs" come in torrents and I furiously try to talk myself out of them. None of my reasons are valid or of any value. Nothing would have made a difference. How can a God of love allow this to happen?

Then I remember. God didn't create sin and sickness. He created the world to be perfect but gave man the right to make choices. Man sinned and so came the sickness. Yes, God allows it to happen but he also provided heaven so that we can see Kira and many others again. Gratefulness takes over my anger and makes it seem pointless. After all, through Jesus we have the power of redemption. God can redeem my anger and use the energy to create something beautiful, something I surely don't see right now. I am reminded as well that beauty takes time. More than that, this whole thing of anger takes lots of trust in God. Trust that I will be okay. Anger makes me feel so unchristian. I was raised in a Christian home and was taught to control my anger. To feel all this anger is so confusing. It is so hard to let the anger come because it feels like sin to be angry at God. But to deny the anger means no growth. To trust God with my anger means to believe that I will emerge on the other side more beautiful. This anger will spur my wound to heal. It's the proof that I am still alive in this pain. Meanwhile, I will stay while the fire rages.

Grief tempts me to bargain with God; if only I had done this or that Kira wouldn't have died. I feel desperate for a way out of this pain. I want answers, solutions, anything that would make the pain easier to bear. If only God would have showed me that she was so sick, maybe I could have helped her sooner. Maybe it would have changed the outcome. My mind teases me. I want to learn this journey, just not this way. Some other way God; I will do anything else. Or if you will just grant all my desires now, I will serve you faithfully the rest of my life. Any type of bargain that God would take would make me happy. Bargaining doesn't work, but is a part of the circle of grief. Believing that something would have made a difference is depressing. I can't change it now. These thoughts feel helpless and send me spiraling into depression. Weeks later I come floating back up to the facts of life and acceptance.

So I am trying to replace denial with God's grace. When I feel it in my face I calmly think of the events leading up to Kira's death and say "God, this is part of my life now. Part of my memories. I can't do this by myself, God. But, with your grace I am okay with it. It did happen and it is alright." Choosing to deal with denial in a positive way points me gently toward acceptance.

And so I am able to stare denial in the face and say "You know, I am tired of being in denial. You tell me things that aren't true, and I choose to replace you with God's grace." I can testify that it is working. Maybe later on God will nudge me to slide another one out. Perhaps removing denial destroys the circle and the rest will need to leave and be replaced with other attributes of God. I haven't figured it out yet.

I had a chance to put my words to practice last week. We went back to Hershey Medical Center and had a meeting with Kira's doctor, nurse, and the PICU counselor. It was good and very hard at the same time. I dreaded going back; the day before our visit God gave us three specific happenings that were totally overwhelming, making it much easier to go back. A few days earlier I could feel that going back was a good idea. The day before we went we had invited a missionary couple on furlough to stay at our inn. The man had a vision during the night. He saw Kira sitting with Jesus. She turned her face toward him and said, "Tell my mom that I am happy."

This fellow had never met Kira. It felt like a message from her for me and made it a lot easier to return to Hershey. Two nights before our visit I had a conversation with a lady who had also lost a child. She shared with me, encouraged and strengthened me. Earlier I had called a PICU, a counselor at Hershey to ask about coming. He was thinking of us when I called. I felt so thankful to God for these three people and for the influence God has had through them.

As we turned off of Route 283 onto the road to Hershey, feelings started to overwhelm us. Marlea wanted the same CD playing as had been on in the van the week Kira was in the hospital. I could feel my stomach knotting into a ball, and Merlin was busy driving. The feelings of fear came closer and closer as we neared Hershey. We were all tense.

Those feelings only multiplied as we walked down the hall toward PICU. The smiling faces of the doctor and counselor warmed us as we neared. They had decided that we could come on back and have our meeting in PICU. Ugh, the sound of the door, the smell of hand sanitizer, and the beeping of machines greeted me like a punch to the stomach. I felt myself rebelling at the thoughts of what occurred in here. I glanced quickly at the six beds in the middle in observation where Kira first was located and vividly remembered the incidents we experienced around that fourth bed. Then on to the enclosed room in the corner where we spent those hopelessly pain-filled days around Kira's bedside. My mind wandered to the patient in there now. Was that patient getting better? Or do they all die?

Kira's nurse cheerfully greeted us and we sat down around the table. We had some questions for Kira's doctor and received the same inconclusive answers. I still just desire answers or ways that would have gotten me out of the situation. I tend to form hypotheses in my mind that would make a way out of what happened. Of course we can't change it now anyhow, but at least that would be a reason for her death. Most of the hypotheses tend to lead me to blame myself which is not right. The reassurance that Kira's doctor and nurse gave me brought lots of tears and freedom for the blame I was imagining. The search for reasons that do not exist is simply exhausting. The situation was unavoidable. In a way that inevitability makes it easier because there is simply no way to associate blame.

The visit did bring back unsettling memories and lots of tense muscles. Later we went to Panera Bread for lunch. By the time we finished lunch, I was unable to walk to the van. I was in tremendous pain for some unknown reason. The combination of the miscarriage, its lingering results, and the visit to Hershey was just too much for me. I sat at the table with my head bowed in agony and then somehow managed to limp out to the van. My heart was bleeding again. The scar tissue that was there was peeled off and the wound reopened.

Going back to Hershey also made us reflect on the faithfulness of God those days in the hospital and the time since. We literally felt as if He was with us in the room with Kira. And the truth of the matter?… He was!

The visit was hard on Marlea, but she really enjoyed it. Not many kids get to see inside the PICU at Hershey! I find myself wondering what all will happen to the imprints this experience has made in her little heart. She hooks up all kinds of stuff to her dolls' mouths. It brought lots of questions again too about all the whys. I was determined to walk into Hershey and be okay with it, and for the most part I was. During this time Marlea was going to counseling every other week. She and the counselor would play hospital. The children (dolls) would all be sick. The mommies and daddies would all be frantic and crying. Then the children would die and the session would be over. Ironically at her next session no one was frantic, the dolls all recovered, and Marlea herself was a lot calmer.

Anna was okay while we were there but was very ready to leave. After her nap later in the day, she spent an hour walking around the house screaming just for fun. I guess it was her way of getting it out of her system because after that she acted okay and happy.

For Marlea's birthday in 2008 we gave her a bunk bed for her doll. But the problem that remained was that the other part of the bunk bed was Kira's. So we decided to be crazy and just give Kira a bunk bed too although it wasn't her birthday. We laughed at ourselves for the predicament. They were happy about it and had lots of fun with their bunk beds the next months. If we wouldn't have those memories would not exist....

like a sponge

No sin is worse than the sin of self-pity, because it removes God from the throne of our lives, replacing Him with our own selfish interests. It causes us to open our mouths only to complain, and we simply become spiritual sponges; always absorbing, never giving, and never being satisfied. And there is nothing lovely or generous about our lives. —**Oswald Chambers**

I feel like a sponge. In the last six months I have been easy to wound, weak. You could press your finger on me and make an indentation just like a sponge. I have small holes in me that would be easy to fill up with traumatized thoughts, guilt, flashbacks, and fear. A sponge is also full of holes; it can soak up any liquid. If the sponge absorbs the wrong type of liquid and is left to dry, it becomes hard; the same also to me.

But I haven't. I have been surrounded with people who have given, and then given even more. Friends have filled up the holes with kindness, scripture, and prayer. They have filled up the holes with promises and reminders of God's redemption waiting for me at the foot of the cross. They have filled up the holes in me with kind, gentle, and soft words. They have taken time out of their own busy days to send me a card or a letter. I have soaked up the words, the kindness, prayers, scripture; my heart has been saturated by them.

One morning a few months ago my heart was especially spongy. It was a wrung-out sponge full of emptiness and sorrow. I was in the bathroom bitterly crying out my heart, trying to hide from the girls. I stood there looking at the mirror, wondering how I was going to stop crying; the water being wrung out of my sponge seemed endless. I prayed that someone would come to interrupt me and encourage me. At that moment one of my friends was taking the road past my house. God told her to stop in and talk with me. She knocked at my door as I was praying my prayer. My tears stopped and I was so excited because I knew that God had sent her. She didn't have many words but they were kind, soft, gentle words. She let her tears fall with me. She didn't stay long, but she filled up my sponge with her act of kindness.

Sundays are especially hard for me. Carolyn, a friend from church, routinely stops me and asks how I am. She is not looking for a response like "fine," she is looking for the real thing. She knows my pain, having experienced grief in her teen years. Likewise her husband often gives encouragement to Merlin. Their care saturates my sponge. I drink it up thirstily but have nothing to give back. She doesn't mind....

I look into people's eyes and see sympathy and true sorrow for our experiences. I let it soak in; I let myself feel Jesus through them. A few months after Kira died an annual sale was hosted in the community. Merlin volunteers at the sale, so I often go for a few hours. I dreaded it and contemplated not going. Stay home and hide rather than feel the eyes and hear the words again. The girls really wanted to go, so I gave in. Last year's memories of the sale seemed so alive. It was just as I expected. Eyes, eyes, eyes everywhere seemed to follow me. Everywhere I looked I met another pair of them peering at me. I tried first to look away only to find more eyes. I tried to look at the ground only to bang into another set of eyes. I tried looking at the sky only to feel my tears roll down my cheeks. Finally in awkward desperation I just looked at the eyes, the people. Sometimes I smiled and other times I chose not to. The eyes my glances met were full of kindness and sympathy. They melted me. They filled up the indentations in my sponge. My feelings of awkwardness slowly turned to ones of feeling loved and cared for. There were also kind, encouraging words. Conversations that will stay with me for a lifetime. I came home with a filled up sponge. My memory of emptiness and sorrow was replaced by eyes sorrowing with me. Eyes that wondered if I am doing okay…hearts that I knew were offering prayers heavenward for me.

I feel like a sponge that will absorb lots of water. I am soaking up the words, the caring eyes, the acts of kindness. There is a cut-off point when wringing out needs to happen or the liquid will spill everywhere. Our friends just lost their seven-year old son yesterday. I mourn and weep for them. I am tempted to stay in my comfortable house. I could say "I can't go; it will bring too much pain and flashbacks." But they need others. They need people who know how they feel. Will I let my sponge be wrung out into another's desert? Do I believe I have anything to offer them? Am I going to keep absorbing and absorbing and never give? Or will I let it come out? Will I let everything that has filled me, the energy other people have poured into my life, the kind acts and words that touched my broken spirit-can I let it out?

So, I went. Merlin and I both went. We sat with our friends. As we met them tears rolled down our faces. The lingering darkness swallowed us as we realized someone else knew our pain and it was worse for them right now at this moment than for us. A raw, ugly likeness to have with your friends. A few days later we attended the viewing. Merlin and I stood at the casket together and cried. We cried openly that night more than we had in the previous six months. It was so hard to see a little body in the casket again, know the pain the parents are going through, know the pain the siblings will and were experiencing. I felt jealous that he was with Kira. It was not that I wanted to die; I knew I was still needed here. I always have a desire to be in both worlds at the same time. In some ways being able to cry for someone else's pain and loss felt good and healing, to give and encourage from the depths of our broken hearts. To attempt to pass on the kindness that was given to us, and to let the water run out of our sponge into someone else's. The next day we attended the funeral. We sat in the balcony in the front. I cried uncontrollably the entire service. My purpose for going was to be an encouragement, but the service seemed to be more of a healing balm for my own heart. To be wrung out and filled up on the same day is the ultimate experience of a useful sponge. Yes, to stay dry would be more comfortable but certainly not more fulfilling.

We were in Ohio to visit Merlin's family over the weekend. It was hard and good at the same time. It seemed okay to go finally. We missed Kira terribly; missing her could seem so raw again. I have had lots of opportunity to put last week's thought to action. But again, my sponge was filled with kindness and tender words. Even Sunday morning at church, we saw people we haven't seen for months; really I don't know them very well. But they genuinely cared, and I felt Jesus through them. I was encouraged. Being with family again felt good, though different.

I will attempt to share my two favorite memories of Kira in Ohio. When we arrived at Grandpa's house, she had a mission to fulfill. Her mission was to find Grandma. We would sometimes arrive late and Grandma would be asleep on a chair. She couldn't feel at home until she found her. Once she was in the shower and Kira had to wait until Grandma was finished. She didn't have lots of words for Grandma, but the beaming, delighted face said it all.

playing with Grandma Yutzy

My other memory is that she liked Grandpa's rug in the living room. In fact, she liked it so much that she would crawl with the top of her head down against the rug and go across the floor like that just to be crazy. It of course made her hair stand out. I guess it was soft compared to our floor! Who knows?

Trigger Points

A new scar is tender. To take a pin and pierce skin would hurt tremendously and cause the newly formed blood vessels to again have to go through the clotting stage.

The wound on my heart is also tender. Circumstances, places, and maybe even smells command me to feel the knife again. They are there embedded into my brain. Time will soften them but for now they trigger me to remembrance of what used to be normal. They trigger my senses to wish to be the "other person." The overpowering instinct of wishing for someone I cannot have rips my wound open again. As if desperate to balance the pain, I remind myself that to feel pain of this degree means I loved deeply. Having loved deeply brings no regret.

balancing

Life is like riding a bicycle, to keep your balance, you must keep moving.
—**Albert Einstein**

The removal of denial takes more effort than I anticipated. My balance in this circle of grief, and interrupting it, is being shaken to the core. Some of the events of the last weeks have intensified my desire to be more real and be okay with Kira being in heaven. By trying to face denial more realistically my longings for Kira have also intensified, which in turn makes the struggle to rely on God more intense. I keep reminding myself that I have chosen to trust God, and no one is forcing me to do so.

I find that by removing denial, the other parts of "the circle of grief" seem to still be at home. I have decided that they are going to stay. They don't seem wrong to me. Anger is part of God. Bargaining can have its place, although the Bible accounts of this don't always turn out really well. Depression is sometimes a part of walking through a valley because when we are low we search the Bible more and seek out God. Life isn't all mountaintop experiences, so ups and downs have their place in the balance. The last visitor in the circle, "acceptance," is definitely a Godly attribute. These visitors are tipsy, and all of them can be taken too far. A gentle balance seems to be between good and bad. Will I learn to live the balance? My visitors in this grief circle, with God's grace, will become balanced. Will I learn when I am tempted to be overbalanced to not do so, but instead rely and trust in God more? Will I recognize the signs of overbalance and stop myself before I get there?

This act, this balancing is part of the healing; our family is part of this scale as well as our friends and our church family. My sister catches me with her frequent phone calls. These calls help bring me to reality. The call that makes me think, "Really what am I doing today? Stumbling around with a spaced-out mind or am I really here?" My parents catch me by inviting us over. Frankly, sometimes I have no energy left and it's the words, "Can you come for lunch, and no, don't bring anything" that balance me back on the scale. My friends tip me gently by their acts of kindness and thoughtful words in my presence. They are selective in their speech in my presence because I feel tipsy. They speak softly when asking me about Kira and my feelings. They gently prod me towards acceptance. Sometimes they talk about how they are feeling, and that helps me realize that life isn't all roses even if one is not in grief. They seem to balance the conversation just right by caring about us and yet talking about other things as well. One couple several weeks ago invited us to a restaurant with them for dinner. They just wanted us to tell them again about Kira's death and how it is for us. It balanced us again, drawing us toward acceptance and yet caring about the past and its experiences that are so deeply a part of who we are now. The flowers and note from a family member on Mother's Day balanced the feelings between this year and last year. These signs of care called me to live today, not last year and yet reassured me that I am okay. I open the mailbox and find yet another card. Someone heeded the Spirit and took time to write us a note. Some mornings when I am doing breakfast just finding one of my guests looking at Kira's picture balances my whole day. Yes, I tire of telling the story over and over and trying to explain what happened to different people every day. But somewhere in that I also find the balance through people's kindness and acts of sympathy. Some nights when sleep evades me I find the balance through the comments on the blog. At that hour when I am tired and worn out they call me to worship the Creator who restores and redeems. I return to the middle where feelings are more even and I can sleep peacefully.

Kira loved to come into bed with us. Neither Marlea nor Anna liked to sleep there, but to Kira it was the ultimate sleeping spot. She usually didn't care if I was there or not; she wanted Daddy. At fourteen months old she was climbing out of her crib by herself. Out of fear that she would hurt herself, we put her into a toddler bed. So of course this was great, since she could now find our bed by herself whenever she wanted to do so. She hardly ever slept through the night until she was two years and three months old, so this was a constant struggle. One morning after a particularly restless night, I awoke with a start. Where was she? I then felt some feet in my hair and after a closer look I found her curled around Merlin's head. They were both sleeping peacefully. I sighed and enjoyed the moment. I often think of those sleepless nights and thank God for them. I got to hold her and spend hours more time with her that way. Sure, some nights were frustrating; but the experiences outweigh the frustrations now.

the grave

To dust thou art and to dust thou shalt return. **Genesis 3:19**

When attending church, we have had a new parking spot. Strangely enough, no one else wants our parking spot. We are often late for church and our parking spot is still waiting patiently for our van. Beside our parking spot is the church graveyard. In it lies the precious body of our daughter. Every time we go to church I glance at that little plot and wish that she would be walking to church with us; wishing I would be taking her hand like I did so many times. Instead, I take Marlea's hand and the other hand is empty. Merlin, Marlea, Anna, and I walk into church feeling empty. The pain is so real and seems so present when we are at the same place as her body. Often we stand to sing a few songs after Sunday school. I glance out at the cemetery and see the little marker. I compare that in my head to seven months ago when her body was right here beside me alive and full of jumping energy. I don't like it. After church we walk back out to our van. We walk over to her grave (Marlea is often already there) and stand there sadly around it. Anna sometimes walks over it or runs off to explore gravestones, especially fingering the angel engraved into a memorial stone close by. Anger threatens to overwhelm me as I gaze at the outline of her casket in the grass (the ground sunk again, third time). I want her. I want to hold her again.

My mother heart is torn. Torn because I don't want her in the grave, but also torn between months ago and now. I don't want to connect them; here at the grave I am forced to do so. I am standing here looking at her grave, but I want to see her here beside me and I can't. Here, at the grave I know it's not true.

My mind wanders back to the picture I have in my mind of her body in the casket. I think of the verse "To dust thou art and to dust thou shalt return." I know it is true but it is so hard to think of the body I cared for and loved turning to dust. Then my mind drifts to heaven and the real pictures God has given me of her there. I feel myself relaxing in the peace of knowing that this is only her body under this sod; the real Kira is in heaven with a new body. I marvel again at God's plan of salvation and the triumph Jesus has over the grave. Because of Jesus, I have the hope of seeing my little girl again. Peace and reality mix as Merlin and I eventually turn around and walk back to the van. My tears flow as I climb in my door. A silent unspoken sadness reigns in our van as we drive toward home; with the exception of Anna, who is often screaming.

Often when I am in the graveyard on Sundays my mind goes back to two weeks before Kira died. My aunt passed away and we were at the graveside. Marlea was peering over the grave and Kira could have cared less about the whole procedure. She was enjoying herself immensely tramping around the graveyard between memorial stones and over a barren, recently covered gravesite. It was wet and muddy that day and her black boots were soon coated with sticky mud. Merlin at one point tried to entertain her on his shoulders. It was fine with her…he was at the edge of the tent, so Kira's head was way above the tent. It didn't matter to her that she couldn't see or that all she could see was the top of the tent. What mattered was that daddy was holding her. It didn't last long and she was soon back to stomping around. By the time we were finished, she was a mess waiting to be cleaned up. Her daddy did the cleanup, though frustrated at her wandering.

School has started and brought changes for us at home. The house seems so empty and just not the way we thought it would be. Anna, though only

17 months old, and not having seen Kira for the last 7 months, often walks around the house on those two school days calling "Kiki, Kiki…." (She did not start this practice until after school began.)

CHAPTER THIRTY

the missing piece

To miss one's child is to miss a piece of you

I often seem to be looking for something. I feel as if something is missing. Maybe I am forgetting something as I walk out the door. I double-check myself; I have my keys, phone, and wallet; everything is here. Maybe I have forgotten to use deodorant or perhaps I forgot to brush my teeth. Something just isn't right. I have this sensation that I am incomplete. Today I was working in the girl's bedroom trying to rearrange everything so it fits. They sleep in one room, so everything has to have a place, or there is no place to walk. I keenly felt as if I could arrange everything, but still have something missing.

It confused me; I know what it is, I know who it is. I cannot stop missing her. It's her I am missing; her jacket I haven't zipped; her doll that is still in the room; her shoes that I haven't tied. It's the one that I haven't strapped into her car seat. It's the one whose face I miss when I turn to look at my girls in the van. It's the one that I am missing as I clean up the bedroom, with her opinions and ideas about how I should do it. It's her dolls that no one is mothering. It's her things that are still in place, untouched for months. They float around and Anna plays a little with them, but they don't really have an owner. It's her stuffed animals that dominate the pile. They lie forsaken and lonely, waiting just like the rest of us for their owner. It's her sippie cup that I haven't filled with water this morning. Her place at the table that is empty.

But she doesn't come; she isn't hiding, neither is she sleeping. Merlin comes in the door and she is not with him… Kira is the piece that is missing. She is the piece that will be missing until we die. We will need to be okay with the missing piece. To learn to be joyful when we are missing a piece of our life is not an easy feat. And so I lovingly pick up her dolls and put them on Anna's bench. Tears threaten to rain as I rearrange the doll chest and put some favorite stuffed animals on it. I remember each one's origin and I smile. Every one of them comes from a guest here at the inn. Every one of them is full of character, just like Kira. Crazy ones, like a brown moose that she loved; a frog holding a baby frog; a teddy bear that could wrap its arms around her neck; a lamb that sang her lullabies when she was a baby; a cute white teddy with a pink nose; a lavender one with a ribbon that she always thought was so cute. A lion with which she and Marlea roared at each other. Almost all these had some time in her bed. I look at them and sigh, wishing she could still play with them.

A year or so ago I purchased some soaps that look like chocolate. We gave them as gifts to our guests for Valentine's Day. Marlea and Kira thought this was big stuff and tried to sneak them whenever they could. Once I left one lying back in the laundry; when I found it again it had teeth marks on it with a small piece missing. Apparently Kira (with her love of chocolate) had thought she found her chance for some chocolate and took a bite. She was so eager that her memory failed to remind her that it was soap, not chocolate. And so we laughed and the girls got one more bar of their beloved chocolate soap. It does smell and look very appealing. It must have not tasted too bad because I never heard anything about it from Kira.

searching to see

For now we see through a glass darkly, but then face to face; now I know
in part but then shall I know even as also I am known. **I Corinthians 13:12**

I am still searching for the missing piece, and I can't find it. I know who
the piece is, but she is not here as far as I can see. Why can't I see? I feel blind,
not able to look, as if beyond me and my human body. And it is, but I want
to smash something to be rid of this blindness. The thought makes me angry.
Maybe I should go on a global search looking for my missing piece. Why do
I have to miss her, a child I loved more than myself, this piece of me? The
longing inside of me is intense; I feel frustrated.

Last night as I lay in bed I was talking to Jesus. Suddenly I felt Kira
beside me, her head on my arm. I cried out "God I can't handle this, take
the feeling away. I could feel her; why couldn't I see her?" It felt too good.
Just think… if I could have her back again everything would be okay and
this nightmare could be over. I heard Jesus say, "Okay, if you are not ready
to have feelings like this that is okay." That quickly the sensation was gone,
and again I was left searching.

I would like to bottle my sin and kick it away; so far away that it would
never come back. Then my search would be over; because if I wouldn't be on
a sin-cursed earth I would be able to see heaven and Kira; then my missing

piece would be found. The curse of sin blinds me, and keeps me from seeing heaven now. I wait in pain for the day when the curse on mankind will be broken and I will finally see.

I long to see what I have come to suspect more and more. I am suspicious that heaven is right in front of our eyes. Our sin, the curse on mankind from the Garden of Eden, keeps us from seeing heaven. I firmly believe one day we will see and ask, "How could I not see? Why did I waste so much energy being sad when really Kira and all of heaven was so close all along?" God, Jesus our Savior, His glory is too much for us. "For now we see through a glass darkly, but then face to face; now I know in part, but then shall I know even as also I am known," 1 Corinthians 13:12. Thank you Jesus for the cross, wherein lies my only hope!

Kira and Marlea were excellent fighters. I often spent a bit of the day solving arguments and fights. Don't get me wrong; there was lots of fun play in between scuffles. At one stage, when Kira didn't like what Marlea was doing, she didn't waste any time letting her know how she felt. She would just pick up a handful of crayons and throw them all at Marlea; handful after handful until I reached her. One day as I was driving, I looked back and saw them holding hands. It was so sweet. Marlea was in the back and Kira in the seat in front of her. They were both straining their arms and Marlea was leaning forward as far as she could. They were both smiling sweetly. I smiled and realized that the saying is true: "This (fighting) too shall pass." The crayon throwing wouldn't go on forever.

the last purchase

If momma ain't happy, ain't nobody happy —**Anonymous**

Gravestone: a mere slab of stone portraying one's life span and simple identity. But as for one's character, a stone however beautiful holds no memories. It seems to mock the warmness of the life that is no more.

I dislike gravestones. I don't want to purchase one; I don't want to look at them, and I don't even want to talk about what to put on it. I would like to avoid the subject. Can't the grave have just a little marker? Actually if the marker would be removed, that would be fine; I will just pretend that Kira's death never happened. Grass can grow and cover the plot and no one will ever know in a hundred years the sad story of our little sweetsy-tweetsy. I just don't want to admit that we need to buy one for Kira. I can't bear reading her tombstone. How can her life be portrayed accurately on a tombstone? How can I go to the graveyard and read "Kira Mary Yutzy" on one of those cold, barren pieces of stone? Just the thought of it brings stony, sullen feelings to my wounded heart. How can it be that this child who made me lose my brown hair be the same child for whom we buy a gravestone? Just eight months ago I could never sit here to type on a computer. I would have had too much help. Just eight months ago that body that is now under the sod in the graveyard

125

was here bouncing around on the office counter. Just eight months ago I was a normal person.

Now it feels like making the last purchase for our little girl will change me even more. To admit she needs a gravestone is to admit she died and isn't here on this earth anymore. Only her legacy, her stories, and her pictures will last. To make the last purchase is tempting me... I can hear the stone being put on the ground with a thud. It tempts me to put a stone on my feelings too.

I awoke this morning still needing to force myself out of bed. If it were not for my responsibilities here on this earth and the fact that apparently God still wants me here...those covers would have come back up and I would have simply stayed there waiting for nothing. My heart feels wounded and lost. I have no foundation. Just wallowing along day by day by what other people encourage me to do. I have no energy for the basics of life. Those basics all feel the same; just things you have to do every day. In fact, I have no energy at all. I am simply just functioning by sheer determination that won't allow me to give up and cave in. Just the thought of being with little people who are also grieving could send me overboard. How do I do this... another day of seeing that sad little face? Another day of hearing the complaining which is better interpreted as a lack of energy, motivation, and desire to do anything; a strange mirror of my own feelings. I hear CD stories of "Laura and Mary," "the Boxcar children," and Bible stories all week, which I am frankly really tired of hearing.

Two days a week Marlea goes to kindergarten. I need to first drag myself out of bed, then help her get up. Then we both attempt to stuff some breakfast down our constricted throats (around the lump that's in there.) And we are trying to get somewhere on time? Some mornings we are a whole half hour late. One morning I brought her back home again. What is the rush anyway? She has the rest of her life to go to school. I want to be with her...she feels like I do. Although being with depressed people is depressing, oneness is felt also. We know the same pain. Many times she sweetly smiles or puts her arm around me. Sometimes it's the words, sometimes just her touch, lovingly and endearingly calling me to live.

On the other hand, Merlin is stronger emotionally but his body is sick, crying with grief and sadness. Throughout the day I often find my mind wandering to how he is doing today. Some days he is on the couch, some days at work. Other days he goes and comes home later looking drained. How will today be? I don't know.

Bright little Anna makes us all happy with her funny sense of humor. Her funniness constantly drags me out of my stupor to the reality of life now. A life that I apparently am supposed to be okay with to live… getting out of bed every morning day after day to take care of my grieving family. I feel so empty, with nothing to give. How can I help others when I myself am lost? But somewhere deep inside of me I feel a stubborn feeling. Maybe the same one that years ago wouldn't let me give up training my pony. Is that what I am doing, retraining myself? Is part of the depression from me? Why does everything seem to hinge on me? Suspiciously I re-analyze the situation.

If this is retraining I will not allow that stone to go "thud" on my heart. I will refuse it; refuse the easiness of caving in to the crashing desire. If not for myself, I won't give up for those for whom I need to care. They need me to care for them and minister to their feelings right now. Marlea needs me to help guide her through this grief. Somehow it feels as if she will not heal until she sees that I am healing. I will not pull those covers up. Until I find myself again I will bear the agony of forcing one foot in front of the other each day. My weak physical condition is no excuse for a hard heart. Yes, I am mortally wounded in the heart. No, I can't deny God and his faithfulness to me, to us. That knowledge will sustain me again today.

Often when I tried to answer the phone here in the office, Kira would come along and climb up onto the counter. At the most inopportune times she would scream or talk loudly. Her favorite thing to do was to plant herself right in front of the computer screen. Then I had to look at her and laugh instead of typing the reservation information. Doing that was a great way to get my attention and way too funny for me. As a child, how much more obvious do you have to be to make your wishes known that you would prefer the attention be on yourself? I would be irritated sometimes but much more often I would laugh and lunge for her; exactly what she wanted.

CHAPTER THIRTY-THREE

places

I stepped inside and am flooded with memories of yesterday

Swing Low, Sweet Chariot—Kira's favorite song

Swing Low, Sweet Chariot, coming for to carry me home, swing low, sweet chariot, coming for to carry me home.

Verse:
I looked over Jordan and what did I see, coming for to carry me home, a band of angels coming after me, coming for to carry me home Swing Low, Sweet Kira-oh, coming for to carry me home, swing low, sweet Kira-oh, coming for to carry me home.

Verse:
If you get there before I do, coming for to carry me home, just tell my friends that I am coming there too, coming for to carry me home.

Repeat Chorus
Swing Low, Sweet Chariot, coming for to carry her home, swing low, sweet chariot, coming for to carry her home.

Places... different places bring different pain. Memories that are entrenched in our minds; unforgettable scenes, unforgettable sounds, and unforgettable things our ears heard; memories that go with us for a lifetime; memories that different places bring carry back the pain and force it upon us. Here... this is, this was, this did happen to us. We are not only dreaming that Kira's death was horrible... it was. Places bring back memories and become real to me again.

On Saturday we were at Calvary Monument, the church where we had Kira's viewing and funeral. As I sat in the pew, I looked tentatively down to where Kira's casket had been. Yes, I could see it in my mind. Just being at the same place brought back memories as if they happened yesterday. The pain threatened to overwhelm me as I sat there and sang with the rest of the congregation "Nearer still nearer, Lord to be Thine." Tears gathered around the corners of my eyes and trickled down my cheeks. Tears, tears.

My mind flashes back to a few long months ago when Merlin and I stood in that forbidden line down there greeting person after person. Kind people sat behind us in rows on the benches waiting for their turn. I can still remember the first face that came through the line at two o'clock that afternoon, friends of ours from the inn. Just two short weeks before that had been Valentine's Day and they arrived with helium balloons, complete with heart shape and "Happy Valentine's." Now, here they come with tears streaming down their faces. The bleak starkness of now overwhelmed me as I hugged them and the tears rolled down in torrents. I can still see the family who brought their children. I reached out and hugged their three year old. And what about the first responder neighbor who came running... I can still see his tear-stained face viewing the casket. Many, many of those tears rolled onto my shoulder, and likewise mine rolled onto theirs. What about the friend I hadn't seen for years that drove from Canada to come to a funeral of a little girl she had never even met? Ah, I can even still feel the arms of another one of my guests who loved my children, comforting and caring. I can still see the exact spot where Kira's nurse from Hershey was standing when I first saw her, she too with tears. Face after face of people with that intention: to comfort and care for us. That is why they bothered to dress their families and wait in the line to greet us and pay their respects to Kira. The tender looks, the rolling tears, the firm handshakes. I can feel the sensation of a handshake from a family who had lost two daughters months earlier. I can feel the people around me who are part of the church we attend. A lot of them are working, organizing. Our friends, these people we worship with every Sunday are crying, speaking words of encouragement to us, and lifting us up in prayer. In my memory I feel their reassuring touch, hear their kind words, and the sound of their voices. The strong feeling in my heart of needing to have them close.

With a jerk I remember that I am here at this church for a wedding and the others around me are singing. Shakily I join in singing "Nearer still nearer." My mind, however, is still running. Why does this song now make me think of Kira? It's supposed to be about God. I don't want it to be like this. I want to draw nearer to God some other way, any way but through losing Kira. But no, I can see the scenes. They are part of my life and I will not lose them. I can still see the faces… hear the words… and feel the hugs of people embracing our pain with us. I still remember the feeling in my heart as I realized over and over again the love other people had for our daughter and us. This place stirs my wounded heart. It calls me to remember the sharing of emotions.

My mind drifts on to the scenes the next day at the funeral. The long walk up the aisle to take our seats on that bench at the front. The casket in front of us…the casket that contained the body of the little girl that I wanted to reach out and hold. I can even still feel the bench as I sat down, and feel Merlin beside me. Even Kira's doll was there with the stroller we had given her for her birthday weeks before. Only now Marlea was in charge of it. The platform where I sang her song for the last time, the sound of Anna crying in the back, my husband reading the poem he wrote for his sweetsy-tweetsy. And then the last look at her body. Holding Anna as she reached down to pull Kira's hair and the look on her face when there was no response… helping Marlea say good bye to her dearest friend on earth…the feeling of horror and wrong-ness that went with it. I can feel myself bending over the casket to kiss her and snip the strand of hair that I always tried to keep back and couldn't. Merlin, bending over the casket a broken man. The lid snapping shut. The casket going up the aisle. The arms of the funeral director's wife (my friend) as she held me and cried, commiserating through our tears. And yes, us following the casket. The strong feelings of empathy we could feel from those around us. The feeling of people wanting to take our pain away but being unable to do so. We are now singing the last verse "Nearer still nearer, Lord to be thine." Yes, it's a wedding, not a funeral. It's just the same place….

And so I sat and embraced the memories… memories a place brings me, memories and scenes that are embedded in my mind, and also memories that are part of my journey to healing and to God. Memories for me that will always be associated with this place.

Summer 07

Kira loved doors. Ever since I can remember her becoming mobile she liked to open and close doors and gates. We have a gate outside our house on an arbor. That was one of her favorite places to play: open, close, open, close. She also liked to open the front door. To her, it was her ticket to freedom. One day she was playing with a key. She tried it on doors but that wasn't enough. In the process she tried it on the front door, got it open and sneaked outside. It was nice outside and she decided to cross the road and try the key on the door over there. That is where I found her, opening and closing the door of the barn across the street, fitting the key in and out. Needless to say, I was a frantic mother and had confirmed in my mind that some children require extra-protective angels. A few more hair-raising experiences occurred, mostly ones that come with little people who are taller than their minds can handle. As a result, Merlin needed to purchase chain slide locks, which Kira couldn't open. They were not to keep people out, but to keep roamers where they were supposed to be.

baggage

Never carry more stuff then you need; carrying unnecessary objects is always counterproductive.

We were on vacation in El Salvador for the past two weeks; as we were preparing to go I searched to find the suitcases. I looked at them and stared. There was just no way I could pack, no way I could pack up with my feelings. They were not going to fit. I searched vainly for a compartment big enough to contain them. I thought of several different pieces of luggage, and oddly enough they seemed too small. As I started putting things in the largest suitcase, I had no room for my baggage. What was I going to do with it? It seemed so heavy and enormous. Merlin packed the rest of the suitcases and no room was left.

The next morning, in the crisp November air, we put our luggage into my brother's vehicle and drove for the airport. As we drove along I felt confused. My baggage was coming along and yet it wasn't packed. Later, as we walked down the terminal to board the plane I felt it following me. I didn't have that free feeling one expects to have when going on vacation. The thoughts and feelings were following closely. I found myself wondering how my thoughts were going to fit onto the plane. The plane taxied down the runway and yes, it was still with me. But the plane wasn't big enough.

I sighed in relief, glad I hadn't tried to pack the mental baggage; realizing I would never have been able to stuff everything into any suitcase. Even if I had tried, the airplane could never have contained it all. I sighed again, feeling overwhelmed with the thought that my baggage is too big to fit into an airplane. Ironically, it followed me even though it didn't fit.

Hours later we stepped out of the airport terminal with my parents. They were missionaries here for four months substituting for another couple. We were so excited to be here and to be with them again. As a child and teenager I had visited El Salvador a few times to visit my father's brother and family who have lived there since the nineteen-sixties. El Salvador to me meant lots of fun with cousins and adventure of learning things about a Spanish country. Merlin had never been here. As the warm tropical air filled my lungs I wanted to forget everything that happened and just be a child again. The bright sunshine warmed my face as we made our way to the car with the baggage in tow. It was a relief to be where no one knew me and I in turn knew no one. If I did know them, I couldn't speak Spanish—so that was the end of any thought of conversation more than "holla" and a few very blank looks. Here there would be few explanations of "what happened."

Driving out of the airport and onto the highway interrupted my thoughts of the last eight months. Even the smells of different foods were a relief. For the next two weeks we enjoyed the distraction of a change of surroundings. Every morning I was pleasantly awakened to the sound of squawking, cackling birds in the trees outside the house where we stayed. Even though the sound was a bit overdone, it was different and interrupted my thought process as I opened my eyes to another day. The pleasant sounds of cows mooing and chickens cackling called me to remember the beauty of God's creation. Yes, even with a vacation, a change of surroundings, I still constantly thought of Kira. But the change was a relief to my worn out body, soul, and spirit. Yes, my baggage followed me, but God's promise of comfort in Deuteronomy 33:27 was also real to me. "The eternal God is your refuge, and underneath are the everlasting arms."

Days later as the plane hit the runway in Philadelphia I was ready to face life again. I felt refreshed, ready to be home to the memories and pictures that our home holds. The distractions had been good for all of us. Yes, it had been our first plane ride without Kira. The flipside was that we had made new memories, been in a new place, and met new people. The language barrier had been a relief to us; the bright sunshine, singing birds, country life, different smells and food had been a healing balm to us.

Kira loved suitcases. To her they meant upcoming adventures. When she was smaller she loved climbing in and out of luggage. She didn't care whether or not things were in the luggage. As she grew she realized she could pack her clothes in suitcases to go away. Marlea had her own red suitcase and usually shared with Kira. Kira would carefully put in lots of things. I always went through their suitcase and put numerous things back into her drawer where they belonged. She was always so pleased with herself for packing. Last Christmas Kira got her own suitcase. It was brown with polka dots. This was very important; to her it meant she was getting older, like Marlea.

A few days later we went to Ohio over New Year's Day. She proudly stuffed many items into it as we packed. She was so happy to have her own that she shone from ear to ear. Marlea's suitcase is red; Kira's was polka dot with a ribbon on and she knew Marlea was secretly jealous of it. Her suitcase has gone with us on every trip we have taken since February. Instead of Kira wheeling it, Marlea does. It's a touch of Kira we take along. Marlea used it for her carry-on on our trip. Tears came to my eyes as I watched her with it. Many questions, wishes, and pain went through my heart.

NATURAL REMEDIES

We all do it. We look around for remedies to soften the stretching, something to make the trigger points less abrasive. We look on the shelves of the local health store, hoping for a remedy to create wonders on our wound. We don't want to see the scar forever; the reminder of that ugly knife that sliced open our hearts on that fateful day. Surely there is a natural remedy that will take care of the hideous mark on our once flawless skin. The thought drives us to look for a cure… be it on the shelf of the store, in the pages of a book, or maybe we will simply Google it.

The cut in my heart hurts too much. My heart cries out for something tangible to hang onto, something to ease this endless pain. This wound hurts so much in its half-healed state. We look around for remedies and seem unable to find any. On the outside I look okay. But inside my soul, the deep core of who I really am, I am still wounded. Struggling, grasping for remedies to get out of this endless pain that has engulfed my being. Spurred by the thought of healing, I am driven to find an outlet for my energy

grief

Rejoice with those that do rejoice and weep with those that weep.
Romans 12:15

Grief is not something we like to deal with naturally. Grief is not something that can really be described or shared adequately. It's just present and stubbornly stays. I have learned to appreciate grief. Grief has become part of my life, almost as much as eating. It causes awkward moments, frustration for loss of words, and inappropriate tears. I can sit somewhere and have lots of tears, not at all because of what I am seeing or hearing. If someone doesn't know me and is sitting beside me, at that moment my expressions can seem really strange, maybe even psychic.

I have concluded that entering another person's grief doesn't take words. A few weeks ago in El Salvador I met a friend I hadn't seen for ten years. My friend speaks Spanish and my Spanish vocabulary is limited, so communicating is not easy. Being understood required a lot of gestures, signs, and wonders. She was telling me about her family just when her little three-year-old girl ran by. Her daughter is full of life, looks "sparky," and has lots of energy. As she dashed by I burst into tears. I had no words, just sobs and tears. My dear friend took me into her arms and held me. There were no words exchanged, only feelings and tears. She couldn't say what she wanted to say because I couldn't understand. I couldn't say what I wanted to say because she couldn't understand me. So we stood in verbal silence, communicating through both of our tears. What mattered to me was that she cared enough to enter my world. She knew instinctively why I burst into sobs when I saw her energetic three-year-old go dashing by. She shared my grief without words but was present and caring. The silence could have been frustrating. Instead, it was a relief. I always seem to have to say something and this time I couldn't because of the language barrier. I didn't know the words to explain myself so I just stood there in silence feeling her arms around me. Suddenly it all made some sense to me; grief is not something to be explained correctly to another human being. It's a feeling deep in the heart and soul of a human that connects by bold love that comes straight from God. My friend simply put to practice what the Bible says in Romans 12:15 "Rejoice with those that do rejoice and weep with those that weep".

As I reflected more on the grief issue the silence continued to become clearer. I gained understanding that it's okay not to have words for grief; the feeling in the heart is what matters. I am overwhelmed when I realize how much people have given me. I am reminded that giving to others is what life is all about; to be a reflection of Jesus. I want to be more like that!

The holiday season's arrival is a difficult emotional time. I would like to run somewhere and hide. Instead I am trying to be brave and get out the manger scenes with Marlea; it has always been a traditional party in this house. Today we set up one nativity set and found it was missing a wise man. Since Kira isn't here to defend herself, we blamed it on her (probable culprit.)

Thanksgiving comes soon; my mind goes back a year. We were at home all day. Our neighbor and friend came over for lunch. His wife had to work so it was just he and our family. The girls were delighted to have him with us. Our friend is a very calm person and always had a very calming effect on Kira. In fact, Kira almost always behaved perfectly when he was around. The girls often played with Rhonda and Barry when they were outside with their dogs next door, and we had become good friends because of the girls' puppy love. After lunch Merlin, Kira, Marlea, and Barry played "Memory" for a long time. I can still see them on the floor playing diligently. This was big stuff to Marlea and Kira… Barry playing "Memory."

outlets of pain

To find a release for pain is to find a short time when one's feelings can abate

Kira had two little friends at church. Janessa is three months older and Abby is three weeks older than Kira. At Kira's graveside, Abby came and sat on my lap. We sat silently on that cold February day. No words were necessary. Together we threw Hershey kisses and daisies into the open grave. My tears ran as I held her, my heart crying out for my own three-year-old. The next day at church she was waiting with hugs for me. For months after that she was waiting every Sunday with a hug, and would often sit on my lap for a while after church. Some Sundays she would have hugs for Merlin too. Nobody told her to do it, she just knew instinctively. She knew because she needed me, too. She was also missing Kira, and I reminded her of Kira. My heart would often break inside; I wanted to hold her, take her home, and make her my own. But I couldn't.

In July, she and her family left to be missionaries in Liberia. Her only request for me was that I sing, "Swing Low, Sweet Chariot" at their farewell. I granted her request by sheer determination. I knew I was going to miss her dreadfully and it felt like another parting. As the weeks wore on after she left, I realized that she was an outlet for my pain. Her hugs, her sweetness, just the feel of holding her was so much like Kira. Abby is also Kira's second cousin, so in some ways she did feel like her. She forced me to stay honest with my feelings. To stay alive, in touch, and to not deny those feelings. But she did something more; she became my friend. I finally decided to try making another friend.

Janessa had a really difficult time after Kira died, so I decided to try to become her friend. It didn't take long; now she sits with me for a little while almost every Sunday in church. She loves one toy I have in my purse. The favorite toy is silly putty, Kira's very own special one. When we went to El Salvador, I let her keep it for me until I got back. I haven't figured out yet if she likes the silly putty, likes the excuse to come sit with me, or because it gives her a connection to memories of Kira. Either way doesn't matter; what matters to me is that I have a friend that is Kira's age. When she is finished sitting on my lap, my heart cries out in pain. For a few minutes my pain was somewhat quieted with her presence. She reminds me of Kira, and helps me to be honest with myself and the feelings in my heart. In some ways, she is a bridge to my feelings. The energy I use in our relationship is an outlet of the pain inside of me. I thank God for Janessa and Abby even though Abby is far away. I hope to be friends with them for the rest of my life.

In the last several months of Kira's life, each night she would pray a simple prayer. "God bless my teacher (Sunday school), God bless Janessa, and Trevor." Then her voice would trail off sleepily. I can still hear her say those words in my head. I often think of it as I lie in the girls' bed saying prayers. How I wish I could still hear it! I can't help but wonder who else she would have added to her list by now.

Today I was moving pictures around and putting out another manger scene. I wished this to be last year. Instead it was this year and Kira is only in my memory. Marlea and Anna had lots of fun helping me and I tried to be brave and happy for their sakes. I feel time getting close to a year since she left us and I want to freeze. Some days I am very fatigued and it's hard for me to deal with life when I am tired.

CELL BLOCKERS

Absentmindedly we pick it. Pull at it. We think the scab should come off but it just is not happening yet. The remedy we had found should be working. It should be beautiful under that by now. So we do it…gently pick off that rough, odd-colored scab that fatefully formed to stop the blood flow. We are greeted by a spurt of blood. Alas, it was not ready. If only we had left it to nature's course. Now we will have another ugly scab and have to go through the same process. Not just that but more probably than ever is the idea that it will leave a permanent scar.

This process just isn't fast enough. I want to be okay again. The weepy eyes seem to have become a permanent part of my facial expression. This wound seems to refuse the healing I am trying to force upon it. The memories still haunt me. Just seems like yesterday she was still here. I have absolutely no desire to experience any kind of joy remotely associated with upcoming holidays. Any determination to be okay is promptly met by another spurt of blood from my heart. Like it or not, I am still bleeding. Yes, my wound has a scab, but any picking whether it happens from my own mind, circumstances, holidays, etc. seems to end in added clotting and more scabs. This healing takes patience. Patience to be okay with these cell blockers who invade my life again and again seemingly halt the healing of the wound. But really, are they? Or is this just part of the process I need to go through? Will I ever learn how to properly open my heart to healing?

CHAPTER THIRTY-SEVEN

haunted memories

Haunted: To visit often, to frequent.

Memory is the retention of, and ability to recall, information, personal experiences, and procedures (skills and habits)

Memories are unavoidable. They are a part of my life, a part of who I am, and a part of who I am becoming. Memories are etched in my mind, even in my body, and also in my heart. They won't leave, even if they are good or bad. Some of my memories seem to haunt me. I would like to erase them, to pretend they never happened, and push them out to drown in the sea. They seem to chase me sometimes, reminding me that I will never be the same; and that is true. Circumstances that mimic the last hours of Kira's life in our home chill me to the core.

This past weekend, Anna had her first experience with the flu. Merlin was gone for the weekend, so I was alone with my fears and memories. As I lay beside Anna in bed, the darkness and memories overwhelmed me. Hours before Kira took her last breath, I had lain beside her in bed also. I thought she would be there beside me the next day too, but she wasn't. I was at her bedside at Hershey Medical Center. I looked over at sweet little Anna and wondered, will she be here tomorrow? My mind raced, flooded with memories I wish weren't there. They are not nice ones; ones a mother isn't supposed to have. The darkness threatened to crush me...I cried out to God in despair.

I felt my hands clinging to the foot of the cross as Jesus reminded me, "Yes, these burdens, these haunted memories; I died for them also. They are not too big for Me; My grace is sufficient for you." I went to sleep, my arms still around the cross. The memories aren't gone; they will never leave me. But God again used the situation to help me face the pain entrenched alongside the memories.

A few days ago I heard Marlea singing, "My Jesus has broad shoulders, his breath is stronger than mine." The song is actually worded, "His back is stronger than mine." I doubled over laughing at that thought because her breath is strong sometimes, and the thought of Jesus' breath being stronger than hers was too much! Later I thought of it again and it also suddenly made sense; yes, Jesus' breath is stronger than mine. He could run a great distance and still not be out of breath. I often feel very short of breath simply from the stress. So maybe I will sing it like that too.

Kira was a Hershey kiss lover. In our back stairway we keep the cleaning cart for the inn. Kira would sneak to it and eat Hershey kisses from the cart. The only mistake she made was in leaving a trail of wrappers around the cart and down the steps. And of course, a chocolate ring around her mouth. A wrapper is still there... no one wants to move it. How I wish I could find her up there again. Sometimes I eat one, just trying to be like her.

The days seem long right now and I find myself not caring whether or not Christmas comes this year. It seems horrid to celebrate. I also dread the thought of memories being a year old soon; it seems if Christmas comes, soon the anniversary of Kira's death will also be here quickly.

christmas thief

Joy and sorrow are at opposite ends of the spectrum.

I am always aware of a thief I have. It's with me all the time these days. It constantly reminds me that Christmas for us this year brings pain. It steals my joy of buying gifts; I wish to buy gifts for one more person. It steals my joy of making cookies; I wish I had one more person helping me. It steals my joy of planning a surprise for Daddy; I wish I had one more person planning it with me. I even feel it stealing my longing to go to Ken's Joys (a store with hundreds of things that make little people happy.) I love to go there and buy simple things that bring big smiles and hours of entertainment. It comes to me and mars the joy that comes from children planning surprises for each other. It takes over and wipes me out. I give up and give in to it again. This thief often causes me to space out. It's too much for my mind, soul, and body to feel. It's overwhelming then yet to think of Christmas. Seems as though that should be one nice day of the year, and this year my thief will steal it.

My thief is grief. I am learning that this thief and the joy of Christmas are on opposite ends of the spectrum of my feeling. To experience them both at the same time feels very confusing. But really, Christmas isn't about giving presents and family time, although they are good things. Christmas is about Jesus and His ultimate gift of His very own Son to be my Savior. The Savior who died for me; the Savior who can take control of my Christmas thief if I let Him do so. The Savior who can supply the grace and courage needed for me, for us, to stay present in this pain.

Last year after I was at Ken's Joys, Merlin took the girls into another room separately and let them help wrap the presents they were giving to their sisters. It was quite the ordeal and I observed with amusement the one that wasn't wrapping and trying to see and hear underneath the door. I can still see Kira there with her ear as close to the opening between the door and the rug as possible, just hoping to get an idea of what Marlea and Daddy were wrapping inside.

CHAPTER THIRTY-NINE

the Father's hands

There is beauty in a scar…I will see it when I enter the pearly gates

My Father's hands are nail-scarred from hanging on the cross. He laid his hands on those rough boards to have nails driven in them. He accepted the "holes" the nails made in His hands. How do I accept this "hole" and allow myself to experience redemption? I feel myself resisting the idea of my life experiencing change and being different than what I thought it would be. I don't appreciate the idea of life being imperfect…I didn't want this hole. If I don't accept this hole, what am I going to do with the scar? The hole without acceptance will not produce a beautiful scar. It will be infected and puss will ooze with resistance. My Father's hands, though scarred, I believe are beautiful through redemption. Alas, not one can tell me how to do this; each wound heals differently. Oddly enough Jesus' nail-scarred hands are viewed as being beautiful.

My Father's mind, soul, and body also suffered tremendously from hanging on the cross. My Father knows what suffering is. But yet, even on the cross God gave him the hope of heaven by allowing him the experience of inviting the thief crucified along with him to "be with Him in Paradise." The thief on the left chose not to accept the free gift Jesus offered him. They too had choices…to deny or accept. Jesus accepted the suffering, giving of Himself for us. Through acceptance of the cross came the redemption for my sins. Jesus rose triumphantly from the grave and we in turn can be redeemed also by accepting Him into our hearts.

Strangely enough because of this hole, this scarring, I feel a keener sense of heaven like a ray of hope that shines through my suffering in this grief. Will I ever feel beauty again in my life, a life that I feel is scarred and ugly right now? That ray of hope still shines brightly. It's the ray that my wounded heart will follow, the ray that daily lends me hope of my pain also being redeemed and made beautiful. It feels as if following that ray will lead me to believe and trust in those nail-scarred hands again. This hole, this ray is a reminder to me for the rest of my life what the true purpose of earth is. It will as time goes on continually direct my focus toward heaven. For now I am afraid that my hole still has a lot of cleansing to do before the scars can heal properly.

Tonight Kira is holding onto those nail-scarred hands, redeemed. Here I am floundering around in unredeemed grief… unable to give it all to my Father even though I know in my heart that is where I find redemption.

Redemption because of nail-scarred hands. I give it… I take it back… I give it… I take it back. The best part of all is that I know my Father. My Father is patient, understanding grief and its process, and as much as I hate it, He is holding my little girl on Christmas. Tonight I picture Kira with her head on those nail-scarred hands. The same head that last year was on her earthly father's hands.

I was looking at this picture again today and thought the rest of you might enjoy it too. I don't know what inspired her to do this more than her genuine love for her daddy.

We all miss Kira so much these days. Marlea wanted to buy her a present and bury it on top of her casket, so it could be closer to Kira. That broke my heart. It's extremely difficult for me to have serious conversations with Marlea about Kira right now because of the pain associated with Christmas. The pain again tempts me to shut down and not talk, and just act miserable. I look ahead and try to see the end goal…that of having a beautiful scar. Being joyful at Christmas? Unfortunately this too is part of the process. Yes, I am still alive. Yes, it is Christmas. Yes, we are not complete. No, we will not be together on Christmas. No, we don't have to buy any presents for Kira. No, we will not see her shiny smile on Christmas morning. Yes, God calls me to be joyful in the midst of these circumstances as well; He doesn't list any excuses that would allow obnoxious behavior even on Christmas.

I may be a doubter or I may be a realist. When I get to heaven, I will look on those nail-scarred hands. I will hold them in mine and then I will feel tangible evidence that yes, He was there with me even when it didn't feel like it. I will know He felt my pain, He knew my heart. I will know He knew my heart desire to do good, to be faithful. Then I will know that He in his mercy and grace cared for me in my pain. Now I don't always feel it; He seems so distant and yet so close at the same time. Until then…I will follow that ray. My wounded heart will learn to trust as much as this human mind can learn in its mortal state. With those nail-scarred hands awaits my full redemption to perfection.

Perfection is what we desire on Christmas. We buy the perfect present, eat the perfect meal, and keep company with favorite people. The decorations are nice, the fun and games inspiring. No work except for the cook. It's the day we expect to be nice…so much like heaven. Except there the cook won't have to work!

CHAPTER FORTY

in retrospect
on christmas

Hindsight is better than foresight

My mind reflects back on the past two weeks; we had our little family Christmas two weeks ago. It was intensely painful for all of us. We tried to pretend that gifts could erase the pain… but they couldn't. It was still there and someone was still missing. It was strange, as if we were trying to be happy because it was Christmas. Yet the thief was present too, stealing our joy.

We were in Ohio with Merlin's family. On Thursday night Marlea started with the flu bug. I was up most of the night taking care of her and Anna (who couldn't sleep.) Christmas day I spent taking care of Marlea, who was still suffering from the effects the flu brings. I have to admit I was angry. Angry at God. Doesn't He realize that I have had enough? Doesn't He get it that I would like to enjoy Christmas to some extent? I had numerous apprehensions about Christmas and what it will be like. They were all dashed and I was alone with Marlea, holding the bucket. I tried to sleep but alas, every time I shut my eyes my brain rewarded me with flashbacks and more haunted memories. Fear threatened to overwhelm me again as I tried to make myself believe that this is only the flu and she will be okay. Those thoughts were not helped by Marlea; she was sure she had never felt so badly and thought I should take her to the hospital. She too was having flashbacks and haunted memories in her own way. She was a little better in the evening and I spent some time with Merlin's extended family.

My mind wanders more; what was the purpose in these events? Why did it have to be that on Christmas day Marlea was sick? Does my Father in heaven really know me so well that he thought I wouldn't be able to handle celebrating Christmas, so He made it impossible for me to even remotely feel like I am? I realized in hindsight that it was oddly nice. The pain of Christmas-time and the fact that I was lacking in sleep made me feel like a zombie walking around on a strange planet. If it was really Christmas…I was fooled. It was the strangest one I have ever experienced. In the end it was an easy way out of trying to act joyful on Christmas day. Instead I felt disconnected from any sort of celebration and even gift giving. So in retrospect maybe it wasn't as bad as I thought it was at the time. I am reminded again that God is mysterious and I will never understand Him well at all until heaven. I am also reminded that my trust in God can be very shallow; life is not predictable; and the flu is mostly not particular about whom it chooses to infect.

Last year for New Year's Day, Merlin's family was together at a cabin. It was a wonderful cabin with lots of space for little people to get rid of energy. The little girls were greatly entertained by running across the pine floors and sliding. Kira thought it was really fun, especially because she had put lots of miles on her footed pajamas and the feet were fairly smooth. She was so good that weekend. She was in the process of coming out of the two's and becoming more of a little girl.

CHAPTER FORTY-ONE

learning

A new year brings new goals, new ambitions, and new priorities. New things I wish to accomplish, new things I wish to learn, and new habits I wish to acquire.

I reminisce on the past year, and I meet a stubborn spirit. The stubborn spirit is my own. I wanted different goals, ambitions, and priorities than what God had for me. I wanted to learn different things and acquire different habits. I am still entrenched in myself. I find myself lacking desire to be who Jesus wants me to be. I want to erase and start 2009 over and do just a few things differently that could possibly have changed Kira's destiny.

I battle and bargain with God…if only You wouldn't have done all these horrid things to me, to Merlin, to the girls. I cry out; why all this pain? I feel victimized. My heart cries and screams inside me for relief from the grief. My head says "Okay God, last January I trusted you for the year and look what happened! How can I trust you again?" My very muscles ache from the anxiety with which I am dealing. Some days the simple act of relaxing my toes is a job. Just remembering to breathe calmly takes effort. My arms are left with teasing imaginations of someone they will never hold again here on this earth. My eyes are left with only mental pictures as simple as my child at the breakfast table… now a mirage…

that floats in front of me every morning and disappears on the horizon, untouchable again.

I scream again, "God I can't do this, I don't want to learn anything more. I don't want to trust You for 2010. I don't, I don't, I don't; I don't want to learn like this." Something doesn't feel right; the longing for heaven intensifies in my screams. The core of my soul reminds me that I am not created for all this pain and grief, hence my tense toes. I was created for a perfect world where there is no pain, no grief, and no empty aching arms. Sin entered the world by choice.

In turn, I also have a choice to make; the choice to learn what God wants me to learn. The choice to be open to what He thinks I can handle. Most of all, the choice to accept His free gift of grace beyond measure. Grace erases my bitterness and invites me again to find rest at the foot of Jesus' cross.

Last year Merlin and I took the girls to the PA Farm Show in Harrisburg. We had so much fun, and of course the girls loved it. As we were going around to the different vendor stands we came past one that sold cowgirl hats, nice ones with strings and pink edging. Memories of desiring such a hat as a child caused me to think they were really cute. Merlin didn't think they were cute enough to be worth the expense. The girls' longing words and the look on my face changed his mind and we bought two hats. Marlea and Kira played and played with those hats that last month and a half. Precious memories and precious hats! Ironically, we don't think of the money we spent on the hats (:

CHAPTER FORTY-TWO

anxiety

Be anxious for nothing, but in everything by prayer and supplication, with thanksgiving, let your requests be made known to God; and the peace of God, which surpasses all understanding, will guard your hearts and minds through Christ Jesus. **Philippians 4:6**

Being anxious is not fun. I somehow have really missed this verse and the practice of it in my life. In fact, when I focus on this verse and it sinks in, I despair. I feel like saying "Ahhhhh!" How in the world can I manage to really do this? Anxiety has gotten the best of me, starting with last summer. Life just had too many piles; I couldn't cope. My adrenaline couldn't keep up. As a result I have adrenal fatigue, dressed-up words for being worn out; or maybe the step before a crash. You would think it wouldn't be a big deal… I could just sleep it off; but it's other stuff too.

In short words I will attempt to describe the effects of being anxious on my body. I write these because I desire freedom and peace in my life. For one, my stomach is constantly in a knot, and my feet and toes are tense and often curled. Shoulders that are normally even are now raised, making me feel as if I'm wearing them on my ears. My arms are just tingling matter connected by aching tendons; my leg muscles are taut, waiting for the next catastrophe to strike. My lungs take shallow gulps of air instead of long, deep breaths. Sometimes I feel like asking them "How about working properly?" I also have a strange feeling that comes into my nostrils once in a while, making my whole face tense up. You know, that furrow that appears with age? Well, mine is like a cultivated field. And lastly, my heart races with adrenaline rushes. Even my head can be tricked into thinking everyday life is a race to win against myself.

This in short is all a result of anxiety. Some of it is beyond my control simply because my adrenal gland is exhausted. The other majority of the problem is because my trust in God is shaken and I am learning to trust Him all over again in another way. The simplicity of God and His plan for humanity strikes me all over again. So simple; just tell Him about it, believe and thank Him, and let His peace fill you. No room is left for me to hide in myself. No exemption clause is given for losing a child, having a sick husband, a grieving child, adrenal fatigue, or anything else. Just "be anxious for nothing." He even tells us how to fill our minds when we are finished with this whole process "Finally, brethren, whatever things are true, whatever things are noble, whatever things are just, whatever things are pure, whatever things are lovely, whatever things are of good report, if there is any virtue and if there is anything praiseworthy—meditate on these things." I really don't understand God, or get the whole picture of this earthly life.

When I get to heaven I wish to laugh at my anxious self, probably in big, sidesplitting laughs. Maybe I will roll around on the soft, well-cut lawn. Maybe I will jump high into the air and come down without a thud. Until then, I want the peace of God; I want His guard on my mind, and then maybe I can work on uncurling these toes.

Kira's daddy is a mechanic by nature. He has a strong passion for powerful engines or those at very high RPM. Of course he delights in trying to teach his girls about motors and cars. Kira understood to some degree, because when she drove her playhouse car around the family room, this is how it sounded. Her motor would start up by going "vroommm, errrrrrrn, errrrrrrrrn, errrrrrrrrrrrrrrn." With each shift, there would be a higher pitch and more errns on the end. What she would have done with a fast car?

The year mark is coming, whether we like it or not. The pain is great and unbearable, but God is good.

CHAPTER FORTY-THREE

my car

Usually a four-wheeled piece of metal that drives on the road, taking occupants to their destination. The occupants might be short or tall, thick or thin, tough or beautiful, loud or quiet. Whichever they are, whoever they are; they ride in their appointed seats to the destination.

I live in a manner similar to driving in a car. I have become aware of some passengers that I don't like that are riding along with me. I never invited them to ride with me. They seem to just have "happened."

Sometimes I find one or the other to be in control. Stubbornness and determination are two of my passengers. Stubbornness rides in the front. Occasionally I forget to strap in stubbornness, and he bounces around inside the car, bumping into determination. At other times I strap him in place and he sits staunchly with his face set, looking straight ahead, and living out just what I expect of him. Being bull-headed is his definition. He makes all kinds of comments to me as we ride along. Some of them are encouraging, convincing me that I could be someone I am not. Others are belittling and I know instantly they are fake. And to think he is my passenger.

Determination, riding in the back seat, feels softer. Most of the time I don't buckle him. He bounces around however he wishes. Sometimes he gives me an encouraging comment. Just simple things like "That was good."

Other times I just feel his encouraging presence. The wrinkle between his eyebrows is not furrowed, his jaw is not set, and he is not bull-headed like his counterpart. He patiently awaits his turn in the front seat, knowing that someday I will buckle him up there when he is esteemed highly enough in my eyes. Being determined actually means a struggle against an enemy. Oh... is an enemy present in this picture? The definition for determination adds to my resolve to make him my front seat companion, being determined.

I continue on my drive down the road of life, squeal around a corner and stubbornness nearly lands on me; I must have forgotten to secure him. I collide with the bank on the side of the road and determination flies forward, landing on top of stubbornness; and I sigh in relief, glad that stubbornness got squashed. I could go on describing this drive. Several things you may note: first, I can't hide the fact that I have been a mechanic's wife for nearly ten years, and some things are starting to wear off on me; secondly, this is a battle. Thirdly, I am determined to make stubbornness take the backseat; maybe eventually determination will just nudge stubbornness out the door. My car might even drive over him. For now, this is a journey on which I would like to include determination and not stubbornness.

When Kira was about two months old, I noticed she was watching something. She watched Marlea, and mostly Marlea's dollhouse. The watching intensified as she grew older. As soon as she could move, she would writhe in the direction of the dollhouse. Marlea was very particular about her dollhouse; since she is the oldest and the only child before Kira, she was used to playing however she liked. By the time Kira was able to roll, she would roll toward the dollhouse. Soon after that, at five months old she started wiggling. And of course, to Marlea's sheer terror, started wiggling toward her dollhouse. Of course shrieks followed Kira's first discovery about how to irritate her sister. The wiggling continued and she was soon wiggling all over our apartment. She cleaned my floors; her clothes were dirty from the chin to the toe. After she would tire of wiggling she would pick up her toes and roll. Unfortunately a computer hard drive failure caused the loss of all the pictures of those several months. She was just lots of fun!

ACCEPTANCE

So, one day I look in the mirror. I trace my hand over the scab. It has bumpy portions still slightly attached but loose, still connected to a few blood vessels that are not completely healed. I gaze at it, fascinated by the way the shape of it is oddly like the knife that cut it open months ago. The wound clearly indicates something happened; something penetrated deep inside this skin. The tissue around the edges is still soft and tender and could easily be wounded if not protected. Oddly enough it is beginning to look okay.

I feel it coming. Something is changing. Is it me or is it my surroundings? I am curious. I run to the mirror. My mind automatically flashes back twenty-six months ago, two days after the funeral. The feeling that I have changed, I am different washed over me. The furrows in my brows...the red-streaked eyes... the tear-stained face. More vivid is the feeling and look I saw on my own face of wanting to go back to bed, pull the covers over my face, and simply stay there pretending to have vanished. But today, this week, my face reflects something else. This wound on my heart is beginning to feel accepted. My fingers trace it over my heart. Yes, it is still bumpy, yes it is still tender around the edges, and still needs protection. I glance in the mirror; my eyes look alive again. There is light in them. Could it be that this wound, this journey of healing is starting to be a part of my life? I wonder what would happen if I would step in that direction? God is prodding me, nudging me ever so gently, then some days boldly daring me to pursue this feeling. And I follow, not because my heart is in it the whole way, but because God promises me He will walk with me. Besides, why not take a dare? Dare to recognize her birthday. Dare to celebrate joyfully her home-going anniversary. Dare to embrace the pain it will bring and be okay with it. Dare to not care if it takes me down farther. I've done crazy things before by taking dares; I might as well give it a try. The staring into the mirror gives way to a smile. I smile at my own smile and a tear slides down my cheek. But the smile looks and feels nice.

birthday with an invisible person

In 2010 we learned for the first time what it is like to celebrate one's birth without the visible presence of the person.

Monday's child is fair of face

Kira's birthday is on Saturday. She was born on a Monday, February 6, 2006, and true to the rhyme, she was fair of face. Her birth made us a family of four. Marlea was absolutely delighted with her sister. After a few days in our room we soon had to move "the baby" to Marlea's room upon her insistence. The four of us had many happy times together.

I struggle this week to remain in the present. The past seems so much nicer. Yes, one year ago we were pleasantly celebrating with a happy little girl and her equally happy sister. This year in my mind could just seem horrid and ugly. But, I don't believe that is the way God looks at it or would have me to look at it. But really, how does one celebrate the birthday of a person you can't see? I guess we will sing "Happy Birthday," blow out the candles, and maybe even buy a present to give to someone else? Birthdays are supposed to be the celebration of one's birth and Kira was born, but just isn't here anymore…so therefore we will still celebrate. I find it extremely painful to say, "Yes, this child was born to me four years ago and God gave her a rich, full life. She left us last year and went back to God. I am left with a longing heart and a soul that longs for God like never before." So her birthday comes and we celebrate without her, or do we?

Memories flood me from last year. This is my favorite one. Merlin and I attended a funeral on her birthday. We had a babysitter so we didn't have to take the girls along; so after the funeral we took advantage of it and went to Toys'R'Us. We were a total mess. I had never agonized so much over what to get for a child's birthday. Merlin acted similarly and we were laughing hysterically at each other. When we finally left we had two big boxes. We decided to pretend that the one was from Marlea and Anna. I remember going out to the car and saying to Merlin "By the time this child turns 21, she will be expecting a house on her birthday." Kira loved her gifts with all her heart. She played a lot with her stroller and highchair those next two weeks and was sweetly proud of them.

To say "Blessed be Your name" this week is especially difficult.

bitter cake

The words sharp, acrid, and unpleasant should not go with the word "cake".

Saturday was Kira's birthday. In an attempt to do something nice, I made a cake. The recipe called it flour-less chocolate cake. I wanted to try it; somehow the thought of making a really different cake appealed to my aching heart.

I also thought I could enlist some help from the girls. In my perception, these little girls were behaving strangely and needed some distraction. It was snowing outside so our neighbor girl, Maria, was over to play. (Maria is nine and had spent countless hours playing and entertaining Kira. Kira in turn had loved and admired her greatly). Three chairs were lined up in a row in the family room. Marlea and Maria, with a third girl joining them (in one-year-old snatches) were just sitting in the family room; I couldn't get them interested in anything. I had tried games, etc. Surely they would be interested in baking a cake. Claiming to be playing airplane they sat solemnly, silently, and straight in their chairs. Marlea on the right, Anna in the middle, and Maria on the left.

I walked into the living room and asked, "Hey, does anybody want to help me bake a cake?" in my most cheerful voice. I felt fake inside but it was worth a try. After all, it looked to me as if all they were doing was sitting stoically looking at the wall. "No" the answers came very flatly, with absolutely no emotion. "Whatever are you thinking about?" I queried. Marlea replied "Kira." It was too intense for Anna; she ran away. Maria said matter-of-factly in a monotone voice "nothing." I soon discovered that no pushing, tempting, or persuasion would convince them to help me make a cake. I reasoned to make my own cake. I poured and stirred. It seemed really different, but I liked it. No sugar except for a half cup of rapadura, salt, eggs, and cocoa. I surely didn't mind skipping the sugar; the year hasn't been sweet anyhow. Later, I made a sugarless chocolate sauce for icing it.

That night I proudly served the cake. I tried to be happy about it. Nobody sang "Happy Birthday" because we didn't think it fit. We all solemnly bit into our pieces. They looked nice with a beautiful chocolate sauce drizzled over the top, completed with Merlin's homemade yogurt. The first bite tasted really different. Second bite seemed kind of good. By the third bite I had my prognosis: bitter. The cake I had labored to make all this time was bitter. Suddenly, the last moments of Kira's life came pouring over me. The last year's memories came in torrents. The pain seemed to raise my fork automatically and a fourth bite was in my mouth. I chomped it victoriously. Yes, this cake is bitter but I can eat it. Yes, this last year was bitter, but I survived it. Yes, the pain of losing Kira was so bitter, but so is this cake; I swallowed a fifth bite. Until I was finished the cake was actually good. I wonder if this is this how my pain will be... will it be sweet in the end? I don't think the other individuals in my family appreciate my bitter cake. I still faithfully eat a piece every day; and it does seem to get better every day. Is it the cake or is it me? I don't think I will ever know. Will this bitter cake of pain ever be sweet?

I don't know that either, but I know God has a lot more foresight than I have. Until I am blessed with more foresight... I will eat more slices of bitter cake drizzled with bitter sauce. As for little girls that stare at walls together in silence; the level of sympathy that I felt being passed from Maria to Marlea was indescribable. It was a sacred experience!

After Kira's third birthday she soon discovered that Anna fit nicely in her birthday stroller. They went on walks through the house in a procession of the three of them; Marlea wishing to be pushing, Kira proudly pushing, and Anna happily riding. They did it with the old stroller too and I wish to have a picture with the new stroller.

incidents

The little things that "hit" you like a brick out of nowhere

Sometimes reality hits me hard and gets right in my face. It chills my heart, freezes my brain, and sends darts to my soul. Pain that is just so hard to realize and cannot be fully described with words.

One night I was giving Marlea and Anna a bath. We accidentally put three washcloths in the bathtub. Marlea stared at it and said "I wish Kira would be here to use that washcloth. If she would be here then everything would be okay again. It's so hard this way." Feelings raced up inside me screaming in pain. I was tempted to feel tortured, ruined forever.

A few days later on Valentine's Day, I was dressing Anna. I pulled out some tights with hearts on them. My memory said there is another pair that might still fit Marlea. I should have known better… I dug a little and pulled them out. The tag said 4T-5T. I fingered them lovingly and shoved them back into the drawer. How I would have loved to put them on Kira.

Again those torturous feelings screamed inside me causing me to feel inexplicable, unbearable pain. My soul takes me to the foot of the cross and I hang on knowing that Jesus felt my pain. The gratitude I feel in my heart for His sacrifice so that I can see Kira again is also beyond words.

Last Valentine's Kira, Marlea, and I had a lot of fun making sandwich cookies for our inn guests. Marlea helped for a while, then she was ready to move on to something else. Kira helped me to the end, including helping me put the cookies into little boxes. I was surprised; she was so grown up about it and really was helping. I still have the recipe stuck on my kitchen cabinet. It was the last thing she helped me to bake. If you ate one of those cookies, consider yourself fortunate (Kira and her Papa especially enjoyed eating any available ones) and know that a little girl delighted in helping make them.

We cross the year mark on Friday that Kira went to the hospital. Please pray that our feelings could continue to be redeemed. Thinking of those memories has gotten somewhat easier and yet they still are like I wrote: deep pain beyond description. We want to rest in God and His plan for us and our family.

awkwardness

Awkwardness is an unpleasant feeling, which can often arise in tense atmospheres when one doesn't really know how to act. Awkward situations can later cause a form of anxiety.

Pain is awkward, and no way exists to get around it. It can tongue-tie a person, make words come out wrong, and create brain-freeze. It's the feeling often pushed aside, pushed around, or tried to drown out somewhere. It can cause us to avoid people if a need arises to express or give sympathy. We come up with all kinds of ways to avoid the situation. We don't like things that are awkward; they make us feel uncomfortable. We are afraid, out of our element.

God didn't make humans to experience pain. Experiencing pain and relating to pain do not come naturally. Pain is uncharted territory in humans, and we prefer to leave it like that. Breaking through emotional pain can be like jumping off a cliff. To stare at it headlong feels strange and uncomfortable. Then yet, each person processes pain differently; so what works for one might not work for others. For some of us, the presence of pain makes tears feel awkward. Others are afraid to confront pain because of the awkwardness it might bring in actions; still others are afraid of the words they might speak in awkward situations. I have often avoided deep pain in my own life, and avoided people I knew were experiencing deep pain. Nothing ever takes the awkwardness of pain away completely.

However, ways exist to be okay with pain and being okay with being awkward. I have experienced a lot of situations where people confronted pain and diminished it's awkwardness by talking, by actions, and through tears. Knowing that the body of Christ (church and friends) experiences pain with you can take away the awkwardness of it. There is so much power there that pain becomes tangible and soft. This life as a Christian, this body of Christ, is one that will always fascinate me. The people that dare to be okay with awkwardness because they love us are a touch of Jesus to me. No explanation exists besides Jesus. It's Jesus himself who took pain and turned it into something beautiful, not awkward. It's Jesus that replaced death with life!

We experienced this swap on Sunday. For those of you who didn't witness the occasion, we had a celebration for Kira here at our house. I felt awkward about it, and kind of scared; I mean, what really was I going to say to everyone? My sister kept asking me what plans I had made and I had none. We gave out one hundred invitations to neighbors, church friends, and people that have been part of our lives the last year. Merlin and I decided trying to stuff the awkwardness of it was useless, so we were just going to be okay with it. After all, how do you make something okay that is awkward? By just staring at it and accepting its awkwardness. On Sunday, I did not feel awkward at all. I felt loved, encouraged, and lifted up. The commemoration/celebration was a drop-in from 2-5 p.m. Our house was filled to the brim. The pouring out of love and sympathy we again felt was overwhelming and very encouraging.

One of my conversations was with the ambulance personnel that transported Kira. Talking with them again was very healing. They told me exactly how it was and the terrible feelings and flashbacks they had from the experience. I felt honored that they cared so gently for our daughter. They too struggled with feelings like: if we would have done this, maybe it would have helped. The ugly truth for them too is that nothing would have made a difference. It made me feel more normal to realize that they second-guess themselves and think about that morning also. I felt so blessed by their kindness in coming and taking time to talk about it together and also with me. Talking about it frankly helped me release some feelings that were still inside me.

We had a children's hour with face-painting and balloon twisting. Generous individuals donated themselves and their talents to fill little hearts with cheer. I felt God strongly calling to embrace the children. Engaging the children was difficult for me; something that I would have liked to avoid. It hurt to see Kira's friends and children her age at our house having fun. I wanted to keep them, and claim them as my own. I wanted to deny that Kira ever lived just to get away from the pain. In the end, embracing something that is so painful to me feels like a release of my emotions. We also set off balloons outside in memory of Kira. Watching them drift up into the sky was bittersweet.

Our memories of last year this time are very real to us. In retrospect, I am very thankful that Merlin and I chose to stay present and close to God those days in the hospital and later. The awkwardness of pain was real then as well. I have some good memories along with the bad and I am thankful for them, and also thankful for the friends, family, and staff at Hershey. You all looked pain in the face with us then also and supported us so well. We remain forever grateful.

One of the last days Marlea and Kira played outside last winter they played in the mud. I was over in the inn office and Kira wanted me. She went inside and saw I wasn't there, so she went back out (leaving heavy mud tracks) and came around the front onto the inn patio (leaving more heavy mud tracks) and into the lobby. The dear girl was trying not to make more tracks. What can one do when you can't get your boots off and can't find your mommy? I thanked her for her consideration. She was so sweet about it.

CHAPTER FORTY-EIGHT

the bottom

He lifted me out of the pit of despair, out of the mud and the mire. He set my feet on solid ground and steadied me as I walked along. **Psalm 40:2**

I feel as if I am at the bottom. This past week has been difficult in some ways, but strangely in other ways it wasn't much worse than any other week. It took me a while to be okay with that feeling. Actually saying that to my friends who asked me how I am felt so humbling. I don't have any strength left to grieve, no more energy to exert, no more emotions to feel. The knife feels nearly as strong as it did a year ago, except that now it comes and goes instead of being constant. Is there more left under the bottom for me? I don't know.

This I do know: here at the bottom in this valley I can offer my altars of praise to God for simple pleasures of life. My altars consist of being needy and empty before God, thankful for His care for me, praising Him for His grace and goodness in my life, and the rest He has to offer me continually. This valley is increasing my faith, building up my trust in God, and continuing to set me on a rock, a firm place. The mountaintop seems very far away and I have no strength to think of climbing to it. Here at the bottom in this valley I will stay until I am healed as much as I can be here in this world. Or who knows; maybe the healing takes place on the mountaintop? I continue to marvel about the mystery of God; He has become even more mysterious to me here at the bottom. Psalm 40:2 "He lifted me out of the pit of despair, out of the mud and the mire. He set my feet on solid ground and steadied me as I walked along."

One day in the spring of 2008 the cats and dogs kind of rain was pouring down. There were lots of puddles outside and Marlea and Kira got the idea that it would be nice to put on their swimsuits and go puddle-splashing. Nice idea, but outside was cold. Not just a little cold, the real kind where mothers who are sane would never let munchkins outside in swimsuits. It was one of those days when I had enough of everything. Anna was a few weeks old and I was still adjusting to three children. I let them do it, swimsuits and all. They shortly discovered what I meant by "being too cold." Meanwhile I watched from the window, laughing as they shivered in the puddles.

worn sandals

I slipped into my worn sandals many mornings for lack of energy to put on my shoes. On a hot summer afternoon they were a welcome comfort to my overheated feet. By evening after a shower I plodded around in them, doing my last household duties. Or maybe I wore them that night we were at a summer picnic. Perhaps I wore them to Costco for groceries. Lastly, I probably slipped them on again as I prepared my breakfast for the next morning before resting my head on the pillow for slumber.

I am a bit sentimental; I don't like to throw away old clothes, shoes, or things from my childhood. I want to hang on to them. To throw away things means moving on, getting older, and embracing changes.

Last week I threw away a beloved pair of sandals; I was attached to them. For months they sat in my room waiting for me to decide their destiny. I couldn't wear them any longer; they made my feet hurt. I didn't have room for them either; we don't have a large apartment. I couldn't pretend that they still looked nice, since they didn't. I couldn't say that I needed to wear them yet; they had served their purpose well. So I closed my eyes and threw them into the trash. I thought about them in the trash for a few days. When I took the trash outside I saw them again and had to squash the impulse to dig them out. Throwing them away felt like being okay with changes, and

I don't like changes. It means embracing a new pair of sandals with which I have no memories.

Memories are what tie me to my sandals. For starters, I bought them with my friend Lenora. That's a good memory because we don't often go shopping together. A few months later Merlin, Marlea, Kira, and I went to Thailand for three weeks. It was a wonderful vacation and one that we treasure deeply. I wore my sandals every day while we were there. Then the countless times I slipped them on and chased after Kira. Kira tried walking in them like little girls do. They were a bit large, which she discovered only after driving some of us nuts by clopping around. When Anna was born I wore them to the hospital and home again. I wore them to many a party, weddings, and many more events. Last fall I wore them in El Salvador, though they weren't very comfortable then any longer. I even wore them in the winter sometimes.

To throw them out to me means moving on. It's the first thing that I actually threw away that had attachments to Kira. My next pair of sandals won't know the joy of running after Kira. They won't remind me of her; she will never clop around the house in them. She will never be along when I wear them on a vacation. I am still missing my sandals. I forced myself to part with them. I need room for new ones.

Likewise in my life I will move on to some degree. Right now seems as if it will always be a struggle. Going backward seems more comfortable to me than moving forward. Just like it was painful for me to throw away the sandals, being okay with new memories that don't include Kira will remain painful for me also. Some of the memories will fade to make room for new memories. The new memories will eventually seem precious as well.

There are some days in this house when I seem to be the least-liked member of the household. On one of these days some time ago Marlea and Kira thought they would like to sell me on Ebay. How nice to get rid of the person who keeps order, arranges and picks up toys, gives baths, and wipes dirty mouths. The thought of selling me seemed appealing to their minds. Oh well, at least it wasn't free-cycle or Craigslist.

CHAPTER FIFTY

bargaining

I will do this God, if You will give me that

I am tempted to bargain with God. This temptation has been with me for a year plus one month now. I would like to say *"Okay God, see me here. I am trying to be okay with this. I still love and honor You. I continue to call You my God. Don't I deserve extra blessings? You took away my Kira and I am learning to be okay with that. It would help a lot if You would give me more somethings. Don't I deserve them? I worked for them. Oh and yes, Kira is gone but You can't dare take anything else from me. I wouldn't be able to handle that. Do something God, make it more obvious that You love me if You actually do."* And so my thoughts go on. A few things I am learning in relation to this temptation are as follows:

1. When the sun goes down every night, God is still God. When I close my eyes at night, God is still God. When the sun comes up, my eyes open, and I determinedly plant my feet on the floor; God is still God.
2. God might have a different idea concerning blessings than I do.
3. My interpretation of God is so unreal about how God actually is; I am blinded because I am human and God is not.

4. Eternal blessings far outweigh earthly blessings.
5. I can't suggest to God what He should do; He is sovereign and knows what is best for me because He can see the whole picture of my life and I can't. I can only surmise what I think the picture might be.
6. Living like a begging dog reaching for a bone is not a nice way to exist.
7. What I consider "our children" or "my husband" or "my things" are God's and so I don't have the authority to demand He not touch them.
8. I don't have an opinion in what I think I can or cannot handle; God's grace is always bigger than my need.
9. God's love for me doesn't depend on circumstances, actions, or whether or not I honor and love Him.
10. At the end of this life when I meet God and finally see His face, this is what I want to hear "Well done thou good and faithful child, enter thou into the joy of thy Lord.
11. I am blessed!

Kira liked to be in the kitchen with me. Sometimes out of desperation to keep her out of my stuff I gave her and Marlea bowls of flour, a cup, and a spoon. Great entertainment and great cleanup afterwards. Meanwhile I tried to find a spot for myself in my small kitchen and could hardly find any space left. I usually ended up in despair with a cake baked and little girls covered in flour. Of course they ended up happy and ready to go play something else again, leaving me with the floor and counters covered with flour. I'd grab one little girl and take her outside and shake her off and then the other. The sweeper soon solved my floured floor and ta-da! I had my kitchen back again.

incompletion

For the Word was made flesh and dwelt among us and we beheld his glory, the glory as of the only begotten of the Father, full of grace and truth. **John 1:14**

I can't get away from feeling incomplete. It isn't something that I can fix. We go on vacation; the feeling is still there. Who likes to go away without a member of the family? We go shopping and buy things but it doesn't take away the incomplete feeling. I would like to scream; but it still wouldn't go away. Our family is incomplete. I watch other families and wonder how it would be to again feel complete.

But then I remember the happenings, and the pain washes back over me. Sometimes I feel that pain when I look at someone who is missing a friend. I am now able to perceive that pain in others. I see the pain on their faces; pain which to me was previously incomprehensible. Ironically they see it on my face too. The act of living fully without being complete is something I am learning slowly. It doesn't come naturally for anyone. Incompleteness is so opposite from the yearning and longing we have inside us for a perfect world.

I stop frequently to prevent myself from believing things will make me feel complete. It won't help to go shopping, buy things on Ebay, or even the thrift store. More children won't make me feel complete. Running away won't kill it, and eating chocolate won't help. A walk might clear my brain but it won't take away the feeling. Pulling that last weed out of the flowerbed will not complete my life. In this sin-cursed world my yearning will never be filled. I will feel incomplete until the day I die.

I know Someone who can fill it and I go there again to the foot of the cross. It's Jesus who can make me complete in this incomplete world I live in. It's Jesus who can make horrible things beautiful and fill me with peace. Dependency on Jesus for this seems strange. It's a retraining of the way I think, the way my brain functions. My earthly body would like to hold my little girl, to see her bright smile, to hear her voice. To learn to fill this tangible void with Jesus is a new feeling for me. We think of Jesus being Someone we can't touch. According to John 1:14 He is full of grace and truth. Grace will fill my incompleteness as much as this earthly life will allow. Without grace and truth I would be empty and forsaken. Yes, I will always miss my little girl but with Jesus and His grace and truth I will be okay.

When I think of being complete, I often think of Sundays. That is a day that families often feel complete. We go to church and usually spend the day together. Kira was such a bright spot on Sunday mornings. Marlea frequently seems to arise on the wrong side of bed. Kira would often be at the front door first, coat on, yelling, "Come on, Mia!" I had a habit of turning around in the car just to make sure all the faces were wiped, etc. I miss her face… it was usually beaming from ear to ear.

the shirts

He has delivered us from the power of darkness and translated us into the kingdom of the Son of His love, in whom we have redemption through His blood, the forgiveness of sins. **Colossians 1:13**

When Marlea was born, she had a hard time going to sleep in her crib. I became desperate and thought maybe if she could smell me in her crib she would go to sleep. So I gave her my shirt. I would put it under my pillow during the day and at night I would give it to her. It worked a little at first, but what really happened was that Marlea became deeply attached to the shirt.

When Kira was born, one of Marlea's main concerns was that Kira needed a shirt too. So I gave Kira another one of my shirts. Both shirts were from Jockey and had the same design and feel. Kira likewise grew deeply attached to her shirt. There was no sleeping until the shirts were in bed. Many a night we had to hunt around the house, empty bags, and go through the toys until we found the precious shirts. They were lovingly stroked at night, cuddled close, even gently wrapped around dolls. When the soft padding of little footsteps was heard in the middle of the night beside our bed, we could count on it that the shirt would be along. If it wasn't, of course we had to retrieve it.

The shirts went along on trips, Friday nights at Grandpa's house, and comforted the heart anytime. When Kira grew old enough for a pillow, each night she would carefully drape her shirt over the pillow. Without fail when she came out in the morning, she would be holding her shirt. If I would remember, I would hide them under the pillows during the day to avoid the evening search and of course to save mom from washing them every other day. When I did wash them anyone would have thought I had committed a crime from the noises in this house until the shirts were finally dry again.

That shirt is now in my bed. Like it comforted Kira, it comforts me. It's a piece that was hers that I can touch. Every night I carefully arrange it under my head. Sometimes I put it over my heart. Many a night I have used it to dry my tears and muffle my sobs. It goes with me on trips, often stuffed in my pillow. It looks out of place in my bed; like a stranger that shouldn't be there. To anyone else it would look like something I forgot to hang up. To me it is Kira's shirt and I wouldn't be surprised if it would stay there for years. Like Kira, I even fear losing it. I cherish it and am obviously attached to it.

The shirt ironically is red, the color of Jesus' blood. Now the color is a reminder to me that my sins are covered by Jesus' blood. My inability to accept the death of my child, my earthly longing for her that will never be filled, my anger at God for allowing what I loved to be taken. It's all covered by His blood. Through His blood I can have redemption from my sins, my inability. Every night I feel clean again as I put my head down on her red shirt. It's as good as it will get down here on this earth. Her shirt reminds me that my feelings will be redeemed.

Every once in a while in the morning I would hear loud screams from the girls' bedroom. After investigating I almost always found the same problem. One blamed the other for stealing their shirt. They felt the same and in the dark one couldn't tell the one shirt was blue and the other red. It created motivated fights complete with hysterical screams, thrashing arms and legs, and passionate words spewing from little mouths. A thing as simple as a light usually solved the gigantic problem, which could have sounded like a life or death situation. Just like the girls needed something they could touch to feel secure when Mommy or Daddy wasn't holding them, so I cling to this red shirt, fervently awaiting when my eyes will see my heavenly Father.

HEALING

When the wound is completely filled in, the scab falls off and new skin grows. This wound is hard enough to be independent, no longer needing protection. The scar is clearly visible but will fade as the healing underneath it continues. The shape will remain. Not fully integrated as part of the body, the blood vessels can be seen under the new skin's surface. Every day it is massaged with lotion to promote more healing. This takes effort but the results are worth it.

This pushing, this prodding, this bumping is causing the scab on my heart wound to gently and visibly float away. I am becoming okay with this idea of Kira not being here. It is gently being wound into something that has simply become a part of who I am and what life has brought me. The scab which was not beautiful is gone, revealing a scar underneath that is beautiful. My fingers trace my heart. Yes, it is still tender. But with more time, maybe more prodding, maybe someone even taking me by the hand I could follow acceptance to a deeper level. My heart feels a newly found freedom to allow the scar to heal. Time heals, I have been told so many times. I could shout, dance, sing... and yet the next hour cry, stomp my foot, and yell. But it is there, the desire for healing, a gift waiting at my heart's door.

> *The choice is mine—*
> *To reach out.*
> *To touch it.*
> *To open it.*

take me by the hand

The wolf will live with the lamb, the leopard will lie down with the goat, the calf and the lion and the yearling together; and a little child shall lead them.
Isaiah 11:6

The Bible says, "A little child shall lead them." As adults, we tend to make life quite complicated. I love to remember that following Jesus is simple, and that all we need to have is the faith and simple trust of a little child to comprehend what He has done for us.

Marlea took me by the hand today again. Well, maybe I should say, took my heart by the hand. She is in kindergarten at school and has struggled immensely adjusting to the school idea. Ever since last August, she has had a health problem of some kind. First she had poison ivy, then hives, and then poison again. In the midst of it she mysteriously started throwing up at unpredictable times. We struggled to figure it out. Finally late last fall after another round of systemic poison, we did numerous tests. As a result, she is on digestive enzymes for her stomach. We had a beautiful reward of a happy little girl again but still there seemed to be shadows. We could make her stomach behave, but we couldn't take away the grief she was experiencing.

All along she refused to play at recess with her classmates. She would not be convinced, bribed, or forced. She didn't want to play. Once last summer she told me "I don't want to play with children that are happy." End of discussion. No other explanation sufficed. A few weeks ago she had a nagging cough and ended up with pneumonia. I became quite anxious. What next was going to plague her? It had been one thing after the other for eight months. It was hard enough for me to relax and not try to predict what she would get next. Still, she wouldn't play at recess. A few more weeks have gone by; the sun is out again and it has been a year since her playmate left her. The last few times she was at school seemed much easier for her. We gave her a challenge. Get up ten school mornings in a row without being dragged out of bed and you will get a pink alarm clock (anything is better with "pink" in front of it.) Now she is jumping out of bed.

The last few days her dresses were a bit dirtier and I was suspicious of her playing games with the other children. Today was the ultimate; she was so excited. They played kickball and she was playing! She was right out with it. I looked at her in astonishment and said, "You mean you were playing a game?" She freely admitted to it. I shed a tear and thanked God for the gift of healing. And so I feel led by the hand. If it's okay for Marlea to play games again…it feels like God is calling me too to be okay with healing. I've tried to stuff it because it makes it seem so long ago that I held Kira, touched her, cared for her. To heal means to move on. It means time has taken place and life is beginning to feel okay again. It means emerging from feeling needy and being able to give again. Healing means embracing the Cross and the joy that takes place in our lives when we surrender our will to God's.

Anna is hitting the two-year-old realm. Somehow our girls have all had a terrible habit of talking out loud in church. Anna is a pro at it; her speech is very well refined for a two-year-old. On Sunday at church I was busy, which felt good again. I will never forget the embarrassment and humbling Kira put me through in church. The men and ladies sit separately and I could hear exactly what she was saying from wherever she sat with Merlin. If she couldn't say it she just settled it with a loud scream that made lots of heads turn. The feeling of "wow, whose child is that?" type of thing. I can't say I care to repeat those scenarios but I am thankful for the humility it brought to my life!

CHAPTER FIFTY-FOUR

a day of remembrance

To remember is the act of honoring a past event, person, etc.

Last Saturday, April 10 we attended a ceremony conducted by Hershey Medical Center for children that have passed away in the last year or more. Everything about me rebelled against the pain of going. Weeks earlier I was to email a picture and little script of Kira as part of the slideshow they presented. I had a deadline and I waited until days after the deadline to send it. I just couldn't do it. Couldn't write, didn't want to send the picture, and mostly didn't want to admit she was going to be on a slideshow of deceased children.

To begin with, driving to Hershey was just extremely difficult. Marlea even put on the CD that we had playing in the van the week Kira died, which added to my misery. I could feel my muscles stiffening, my heart bleeding, and my eyes starting to tear. Merlin didn't feel very good, which pretty much killed his desire to go. We neglected to check the exact location before we left. I am not very good at giving directions, especially to my husband. I go by landmarks such as "turn at the grey house on the second corner." He navigates using street names "turn left onto Highlander Drive." As a result we meandered in Hershey for some time trying to figure out where to go. We finally called for directions and arrived late at the event. Neither of us was in a very good mood by that time. Bad start for an emotional day.

Then we struggled emotionally seeing people again that I haven't seen for six months to a year; important people who were part of my journey to God in a time of distress. This seemed to set me off wrong also. Merlin and I took the workshops offered on grief while the children were entertained or played with; whatever happened. My first one was on "Self-Care Strategies." It overwhelmed me; I was so tense just from coming there that to try to relax and enjoy the music and wisdom on journaling etc. just brought the tears. Strangely enough though, I looked around and everyone else was struggling too. I divided the feeling of common ground into three categories: a third felt good to be with people that understood without words, a third of me felt angry that we have to know how this feels, and a third of me felt totally overwhelmed by all the pain. My heart felt so ripped open again. My eyes refused to stop shedding tears. The one eye cried the whole time, but the other eye only teared some of the time. That made me feel even more confused, that just my one eye wouldn't listen when I told it to stop. I felt so out of control. Maybe that is how God will tell me to heal by letting my one eye cry and not the other? Or is only part of me in grief now?

The second session I took was "Grief Spiral," and the speaker talked about different age groups and how each one deals with grief. In the afternoon we had a ceremony and a slide show of children that have died. Kira was almost the last one because it was in alphabetical order. I just could not control myself. I felt embarrassed. I looked around; lots of others had tears too but mine were hysterical sobs. I was afraid it would mean more questions later, but it didn't. It was just tough to see her picture with others that have died. It was like admitting again that it happened to see her picture being projected. I am getting used to it, but it was so real that she is not here; she is in heaven and we can't enjoy her here anymore. That was the end and we came home again to a house with only pictures and memories of her. We took the scenic route home, but it took me days to unwind.

Before Kira had enough hair to comb, every morning she would get so mad at Marlea because Marlea had hair. She would try to push Marlea off the hair-combing stool and would scream and fume. The day finally came when I could comb her hair without it hurting her and she was so happy. Now Anna does it to Marlea and I smile, knowing Anna's day will come also.

CHAPTER FIFTY-FIVE

God's pleasure

Give, and it will be given to you. A good measure, pressed down, shaken together and running over, will be poured into your lap. For with the measure you use, it will be measured to you. **Luke 6:38**

God continues to remain a mystery to me. I like mysteries, so it works well for me. When Kira was in the hospital and also over the time of her funeral, my brother and his wife basically moved into our "house" and took over Anna's care. It was a gift to us that we appreciated immensely. Anna was doted on, and lavished with love and attention those days. She strongly attached herself to them, and as the days went by would even choose my sister-in-law, Martha rather than me. I didn't mind because I was stressed, busy, and unable to provide the security that Anna needed. Plus it was nice to watch Anna enjoying them and they her. John and Martha love children but had not as yet had any of their own.

When the time came for me to reclaim Anna, watching them encourage her to re-bond to me was heart-wrenching. They did it so well and were willing to step back and be aunt and uncle again. Anna had mother confusion for a little while. Over the next three months whenever we would see them, Anna would look somewhat confused and react a bit although it soon became less and less. I knew I could never repay them, but I pleaded with God to give them one of their own.

Tuesday their wish was granted. They are now a family of three after having given birth to a little girl, Kiana. Martha and Kira almost shared a birthday, one day apart. My due date was on Martha's birthday but Kira decided to be a day ahead of time. April 20th was also Merlin's birthday. To us it feels like a gift from God to them; one that God planned to be on Merlin's birthday just to give us an extra encouragement to celebrate new life and good things that happen to people we love. It feels like a mystery; one for which I have no explanation besides the boundless joy in my heart. My joy springs out of the pain I felt from taking Anna away from them that now is mended with the birth of their own daughter. My joy also comes from the shared birthday! One that will always be a reminder to us of the mystery of God!

In ten months when we celebrate Kira's second year in heaven, Kiana will be ten months old, the exact age of Anna was when Kira left us. Mysteriously, Martha will remember the joy of taking care of Anna for us and the pain of giving her back. In turn she will pinch herself and watch her own daughter, now ten months old and remember how much she wanted a girl of her own. I love the way God's mysteries disturb our patterns of grief and pain by simple "coincidences." It makes life feel rich and sweet.

Kira was crazy and had great tactics of pestering. One of her favorite things to do while I "tried" to sew was to stand behind me on the chair. Any one that sews knows that doesn't work too well. I am constantly reminded of it when I wear some of my dresses. The topstitching seams on some of them are just simply crooked. She would always manage to give me a good bump right in the middle of the waist or somewhere very noticeable. I got tired of taking them out so they are just crooked. I kind of like them like that now.

new dimension

One day Peter and John were going up to the temple at the time of prayer—at three in the afternoon. Now a man who was lame from birth was being carried to the temple gate called Beautiful, where he was put every day to beg from those going into the temple courts. When he saw Peter and John about to enter, he asked them for money. Peter looked straight at him, as did John. Then Peter said, "Look at us!" So the man gave them his attention, expecting to get something from them. Then Peter said, "Silver or gold I do not have, but what I do have I give you. In the name of Jesus Christ of Nazareth, walk." Taking him by the right hand, he helped him up, and instantly the man's feet and ankles became strong. He jumped to his feet and began to walk. Then he went with them into the temple courts, walking and jumping, and praising God. When all the people saw him walking and praising God, they recognized him as the same man who used to sit begging at the temple gate called Beautiful, and they were filled with wonder and amazement at what had happened to him. **Acts 3:1-10**

Something is changing; my desire to heal is growing stronger. When I am wounded, I feel pain. It's good to feel pain because it means my heart can feel. If I feel, I can heal. A certain saying reads "No pain, no gain."

Just like this lame man, I keep expecting something from God, even begging sometimes. I feel as if God is telling me to look at Him. Until He has my full attention, nothing can happen in my life. I lay dormant at the city gate, which is ironically called "Beautiful." Is my pain actually beautiful to God? I feel as if it has crippled my life, ruined me, leaving me in a heap. I feel as if I will never be very useful again. This pain, this healing, seems endless. Every once in a while I get a taste of it as if the healing might come sometime. I can see it coming very slowly. It feels new, a strong feeling unlike I have had in the last year.

When Peter healed the lame man he rose up and walked, praising God. Is that what healing is? Will I actually be able to praise God for this pain, for this healing? Will I jump for joy for the healing in my life, maybe even the pain? Will this pain, this healing inspire me to trust God totally again? I can see it; I can imagine it. It would feel nice, positive; something I would like to do. If I am thinking it, imagining it, does that mean healing is coming?

After Kira died and the grief came I had no idea what to expect. I felt so out of my comfort zone because life was unpredictable, and my feelings were on a hypothetical rollercoaster. God ministered to me every day. I had no idea what the next day would be like. I soon learned that God does know, and He sent me people every day that ministered to me and were tangible pieces of God. He gave me thoughts through the Bible that helped me understand Him. He provided the correct circumstances for me to learn to rely on Him. He gave me the courage to allow myself to grieve and feel the pain. My trust in God has been gradually strengthened and is slowly becoming a vital part of my life again.

Likewise, I have no idea how healing will happen. I feel totally out of my comfort zone just as much as I did with the grief. Jesus calls me to live out of the new life in Him. A part of me would like to be stagnant and needy forever. It's not a God-inspired feeling. It's the feeling of Satan wanting to keep me in one place and in that way paralyze me. It's a battle, one in which I refuse again to believe his lies and choose to continue to embrace the cross and its healing power in my life. The feeling of rising up and praising God is becoming real in my life. I have yet to see the beauty of the pain but I feel the new dimension of healing coming.

Kira and Marlea went through a stage of being very band aid-happy. We would use boxes of band-aids; band-aids healed everything. Kira always had a scrape or a banged-up toe. When she was finished with hers she would stick them anywhere she thought seemed convenient. I found them on chairs, the floor, her toys, dolls, or whatever she thought needed one. Band-aids made them so happy that I decided the fun was worth the expense. Eventually the band-aid use got to be ridiculous, so we just didn't buy any more. Then when someone indeed really needed one, alas, none were available.

choices

I trust Jesus, her Rock of Ages to care for her. He knows her better than anyone else and has the perfect plan for her life. I know she is resting happily, whether here or there. Kira, I love you more than I can tell in words, but I want the best for you.

This past year I have made lots of choices. One of the first ones I made was to care more about Kira's happiness than about her recovery. That was a hard one; I badly wanted her to live, but God called us strongly to that choice. I will never forget that morning I wrote these words above. It was the day after she went to the hospital and I was trying to get things together so I could leave. Anita came into our kitchen, computer in hand, and showed me how she had set up a blog and some of the pictures of Kira she and Lisa had found. She asked me if I had anything I wanted to write. I responded with these words. Realizing fully well what I was saying, tears streamed down my face as I wrote these four small sentences. They were a huge part of that first choice we made to put Kira's happiness first above our own.

Days later I made another huge choice: to embrace grief and not run away. Choosing grief brought buckets of tears, valleys of disappointment, and heartache as I had never known to be possible for a body to endure. I knew I would never be the same again. I can understand fully how dying of a broken heart can be possible. For months and months I felt as if I were swimming with only my nose above water.

Later on I made the choice to remove denial from the circle of emotions. That was a partial success, one I am still addressing. It pushed me closer to reconciling my trust in God and commanded me to accept God's grace. When Christmas came I made the choice to try to enjoy it… a choice that proved very difficult to do within the circumstances. On Kira's birthday I ate the bitter cake for days; I partially had to choose to enjoy it. As the year came around we chose to especially celebrate children by having a party, some activities, and lots of good conversations with people who freely embraced our grief with us. Many more of you have done so also that weren't here, and we feel that deeply as well. Again, the choice to not run away from the pain of the anniversary of Kira's death and also embracing the awkward feelings that it brought has been difficult but meaningfully worthwhile.

The choice to be all right with healing seems to follow me these days. Just like I found pain around the corners, in the closet, running after me, I now feel healing along with it. And it feels confusing. I want it; I want to make that choice, but I have discovered that along with the choice comes more pain. I still don't like pain. I struggle to be okay with what happened. I struggle to accept the last memories of Kira here in our home… little things still set off my memory. Yet strongly and urgently healing calls me to accept it as part of what is shaping my life to be the person God must think I can be. Healing can be my friend versus the other feelings that only seem like uninvited visitors.

I have been digging in the dirt. It reminds me so much of Kira. She loved the dirt so much I even caught her eating it sometimes. Today we were mulching. I remembered Kira two years ago bringing her little bucket to fill with mulch to help her mommy. Anna was born at the end of April two years ago, and assisting mommy is so much more fun when mommy is helpless. Or maybe then Kira really felt needed? She was so sweet about it and such a diligent worker!

CHAPTER FIFTY-EIGHT

waves

But let him ask in faith, nothing wavering. For he that wavers is like a wave of the sea driven with the wind and tossed.

I have heard someone say that grief comes in waves. My mind pictures the ocean. Last fall we were in El Salvador and spent two nights on the beach by the Pacific Ocean. There the waves crash onto a rocky shore. Between the rocks are soft puddles of sand. At night the tide comes way up and the waves crash mighty crashes all night long that spray water into the air and up over the concrete walls, often giving water to plants on the other side. Late that night, unable to sleep I lay awake listening to the breakers crashing. I have never been there in a storm but I think the power of the waves would frighten me.

Likewise, in my life these waves of grief crash onto rocky shore. They make puddles between the rocks. Puddles that with God's help I am trying to keep impressionable. The waves crash, the pain is great, and the water splashes on those around me. People see my pain; it seems to reflect out of my eyes and mannerisms. They can hear my pain with their ears when I speak. They can feel the pain in my tight shoulders when they hug me. Many times people break the impact of my waves that would otherwise devastate the surroundings. I pray that they will learn from their experiences with me things that will cultivate growth in their hearts.

My heart is not stormy anymore. I can feel the storm ending. The waves, although still at high tide most of the day, do not feel dangerous any longer. Maybe as time goes on they will be more like low tide waves leaving only soft puddles in the sand.

Currents in my life trigger big waves…yesterday one gripped me as I looked at Kira's clothes. Today one gripped me as Marlea told me how much she misses Kira, especially when she looks at pictures of how it used to be. On Mother's Day it gripped me as I looked out the window at my nieces and nephews playing. Anna told me she saw Kira out there and I felt the wave go through me. Kira's friend sat with me in church and I couldn't help but wonder what it would be like with three little girls. The wave washed over me as I realized that I will never experience a six year old, four year old, and two year old at the same time. Not with the names Marlea, Kira, and Anna. The ocean seems to be okay with the tides. Someday will I be? My longing for heaven grows stronger…a place with no waves. Only peace.

puddles

He brought me up also out of a horrible pit, out of the miry clay; And He set my feet upon a rock, and established my goings. **Psalm 40:2**

After my night of hearing the crashing waves, I awakened to the sound of a calm ocean lapping at the shoreline. Wanting to stick my feet in the salty ocean water, I carefully picked my way down to the black sand. Some of the locals are watching, I notice; always a sign to be careful. I soon discover tarantulas in the puddles amid the rocks. They too are waking up coming out from under the rocks where they were forced to abide in last night's waves. I am carrying Anna and holding Marlea's hand so my foot might be a nice breakfast. The rocks are slippery...ahh. The spiders look at me with their beady eyes as I gently step from rock to rock. I also notice the puddles in between the rocks. The water is clean, swept out from last night's high tide. The sand in the puddles also looks washed and refreshed.

What is happening to me in this puddle, this pit? While I am in this puddle is the water getting yucky or am I allowing the tidal waves to wash me out, chasing the stagnant water away? What is this journey of pain doing to me? My water feels a bit murky still. I would like to keep it clean, pest-free, and fresh. I desire the sand underneath me to stay pliable enough for the "tarantulas" to be forced out.

These waves, this tide, this painful journey is cleansing my life. As I let the waves wash out my muddied puddle I can face life again. In the daily hum of life it's easy for me to just live. To try to forget the grief that is around me every day. But letting the grief waves come constantly refocuses my life, causing me to trust God as I learn to accept the hole left behind by Kira. I repeatedly tell God "I am confused, I am hurt, I am full of grief, but I will still trust You." When I do not allow the waves to come I grow salty, grouchy, and very temperamental. When this journey is further along my goal is for the sand underneath to still be soft. Soft enough to still be able to become a better person for Jesus. For now I am in the puddle. Maybe sometime I will jump up and stay on the rocks. I jump out every once in a while just to remember what it's like on the Rock. Psalm 40:2 reads "He brought me up also out of a horrible pit, out of the miry clay; And He set my feet upon a rock, and established my goings."

After New Year's Day 2009 we spent the night at Merlin's brother's house in Ohio. Kira was still really proud of the suitcase she had received for Christmas. That morning as we were packing, she packed neatly and promptly. I can still see her wheeling her suitcase out to the door for her daddy to load into the truck. The pride was written all over her face. After all, she was the first one to have her suitcase there from a family of five. I am human... I wish....

the third dress

Working with one's mind is therapeutic, as is creating things with your hands

I have been sewing. These dresses I made took way too much time and were too much work. As usual, I got carried away and made too many mistakes; ripped open too many seams, and pulled the thread out of the needle too many times. I found myself quite frustrated at times.

Many interruptions and lots of help that I didn't request (once I caught Anna headed toward her dress with scissors) added to my frustration. My dream of finishing with them in one day proved too lofty a goal for me and instead turned into weeks. Amid all these feelings I am stifling the urge to make a third one. I wish so badly there would be someone to wear it. She would look so cute in it… my mind wanders trying to imagine how she would look by now, how tall she would be, how she would act. Would her hair still be brown or would they be more reddish by now? How much smaller would her dress be than Marlea's? Marlea always dances and prances around; would Kira dance and prance with her? Yes, of course she would… my brain teases me with how it might be.

My mind is cut off by the pain introduced by these thoughts. It feels the pain of reality, the pain of never knowing these things, the pain of it only being imaginations.

I turn back to reality and my sewing problems don't seem so big any longer. It really didn't even take that long to make two dresses. I didn't mind picking out those seams; in fact it would have been nice to pick out seams on a third dress. I would have enjoyed entertaining a third little girl while I "tried" to sew. I would have liked to solve the fights that would have been my "interruptions" in the other life. The joy of sewing the third dress will remain untouchable, and only a dream. The joy that comes from a happy little girl in a new dress will never be mine to experience. But, I will treasure the two that I have to sew...my pain will not steal my joy.

By our door on the wall is the last dress I sewed for Kira. It was the first dress I sewed with my new serger. She was extremely happy with it and Marlea was very jealous. After all, Kira was the only one that had a black dress like mommy. She only wore it two or three times... it will remain a treasure to me.

around
the corner

It is the corner that holds the mystery of the hallway and its surroundings in tow.

I never visited a funeral home before last Saturday. I really had no idea what everything looks like. Those of you that were at the viewing and funeral for Kira will remember the funeral directors, Jeff and Debbie Naugle. They are longtime friends of ours, since about eleven years ago. They also frequently stay here with us at Olde Homestead Suites. About four months before Kira died we visited them. Our purpose was to check out the "creepy house" they had on a piece of property on which they were planning to build a new funeral home. The house was going to be demolished and Merlin wanted to check about salvaging some lumber. So we toured the "creepy house" with them. The girls loved it and both found some treasures to bring home. A few weeks later Merlin and Barry ripped out a bit of lumber which is being turned into flooring.

Last Saturday they invited us to tour the new funeral home. I fought with God on the way there. I wanted to go back to how life was earlier. I didn't want to know the pain of a funeral home, I didn't want to drive on those roads without Kira, and I didn't want to even go past the restaurant where we had eaten supper that night. I struggled with the lonely feeling… the kind where I drive down the road looking at people's faces wondering if they know what pain is like or if it's just me. I felt angry at the fact that what should be three little girls riding in our van was only two visible ones. My thoughts were turning into a rambling of "wishes" for the "other life."

So we drive into the lane. The remnants of the "creepy house" are now buried under the parking lot. Jeff and Debbie meet us as we enter. I am still feeling overwhelmed and angry. As we go into the hallway and around the corner I stopped short. On the wall is a beautiful, large picture of the little girl I am missing so badly today. The photo is of Kira opening the gate on the arbor in front of our house. My anger melts to tears as I realize the care and love of the people walking beside me. I am not alone; others feel this pain too. They too want to remember her, to honor her, to make her live on in people's hearts. On the bottom of the picture are words to this extent: "Kira Mary Yutzy; our children's room is dedicated in her honor." The next doorway past this picture is a playroom for children.

My mind continues to race as I realize again the gift they gave us in caring for Kira after she died. God again showed me his everlasting love for me through them. Things like this don't just happen because others make them happen. Things like this come out of a pure love for God. To feel God's love through other people is a powerful effect of a Christian's life. In turn my aching heart was calmed. I was able to enjoy our time with them touring their funeral home we had heard about for years. Later on Debbie took me into the back and explained to me some of the process of embalming. Mostly we talked about how it was for them to work with Kira's body. It was a place in my mind that was untouchable before this, but always made me wonder. Of course I had no idea that they stayed up together that night; never stopping until they were finished, which was about 4 a.m. Never had it dawned on me that when we were making funeral plans with them the next morning they had only gotten about three hours of sleep. I was overwhelmed with gratefulness for their care of Kira. It also opened my mind to a world I didn't know about before. I have great admiration for people who choose this profession and embrace the pain that enters with it. I personally will remain grateful for the rest of my life. The gift they gave us is priceless; that of their care, but also of their hearts.

The earlier occasion when we went out for supper with Jeff and Debbie holds one of those memories I won't forget. I was busy with Anna and Merlin was busy with Marlea so Jeff was holding Kira. I don't remember that she had much to say to him or he to her, but the picture remains embedded in my mind. I often think of it when I think of them caring for Kira after she died. It causes me to realize that someday everything will be perfect again.

THE SCAR

Scars are areas of fibrous tissue that replace normal skin after injury. A scar results from the biological process of wound repair in the skin. Thus scarring is a natural part of the healing process. With the exception of minor lesions, every injury results in some degree of scarring. The point of the ugly knife as it cut away the layers of skin is embedded into the shape of the scar. My body remembers clearly how it felt. With time it will change and fade but never leave completely.

I run my hand down over the scar on my heart; it is long, ugly, and deep. Tinges of pain bring reminders of the clotting, scab, and healing. The scar will be with me for life, tangible evidence of trauma that has been refined and healed. With time, like a skin wound, it will change and fade but will never leave completely. To a passerby it might still look like an ugly scar. It does to me most days. But some days, the bright ones, I get a glimpse of something. Beauty, growing trust, and an understanding of God like never before. Would I want to be "the other person?" Yes, I still desire to have Kira here. But no, I don't desire to be who I was before this happened. To be without what I learned and am still learning from this wound would feel disappointing. This wound has changed me, molded me into a gentler person than before. Those rough edges where the knife cut crooked, the clotting, the scab, the desperate search for a remedy, the stretching, and finding the bottom. These have become part of who I am. As time goes on my desire for Kira remains the same. But with time the terrors that contributed to this scar will fade. My heart will thump less when things "trigger" thoughts related to the incident. The things that will not fade are the life lessons I have learned. God will continue to beautify this wound causing me to grow, change, and become more like Him. And strangely, out of the wound I feel energy. Energy to do good in the world, in my family, among my friends, and to other people who are hurting.

> *This gift is borne in my own pain*
> *I am holding it.*
> *Touching it.*
> *Embracing it.*

traveling with stuff

There is always room for one more thing, one more feeling to stuff in and take along for the ride.

We packed up our stuff; literally "stuff" stuffed into a truck and tied onto the back. It's that time again... time for family vacations. It's the time when happy families go spend time with each other. Time to discover nieces' and nephews' latest antics; time to catch up on the last six months of family living out-of-state; time to welcome the latest additions to the family. As we drive with our "stuff" and two children my mind drifts. Where would Kira be sitting amidst this "stuff?" What would she be saying? What would have she packed in her polka dot suitcase? Where would she sleep? And yes, I am "stuffing" my feelings in this truck too. Tying them down on the back, roof, inside, wherever there is a crack. I feel myself sinking as I realize that my brothers' and sisters' families will be complete this weekend and ours will not. I will again be faced with choices. I can choose to ignore any child close to Kira's age or choose to be okay with them and embrace the pain caused by the "hole" in our family. I feel thankful that it is not last year and that we are driving to a different cabin.

After two hours of driving we arrive at our destination. Up a winding hilly lane to a beautiful clearing and a cabin that would better be termed a modern type of "cabin." Of course the first little people I spot are the bouncing four-year-olds waiting for their next adventure. There are two boys six months older than Kira and one girl six months younger than Kira in our extended family. My eyes linger over them, wishing for a four-year-old of my own. All weekend I watched them and all weekend I wondered what Kira would be doing. I concluded sometimes she would have been with them and other times with the "older" girls and Marlea. Wonderings that will never be satisfied; thoughts that will remain unknown to me; longings that will never be filled. The adults always have a time in the evenings to catch up on the latest in our lives. Mine will be about the same: morbid pain dripping from my tense lips. But I have to admit; it's not all about pain anymore. It is mixed up with some good stuff and really the pain is just becoming part of my life. There are some good things: the coming baby in November, Merlin's improved health, the joys of raising two girls, and the joy of feeling true healing.

Still this life of incompleteness is an art to live. I can choose to just "live" or I can choose to be joyful while I live with my unfulfilled longings. I must realize that this earth is imperfect, that wonderings will continue to be only wonderings, and that longings will only be filled to perfection in heaven.

Two years ago when we were at the mountains I got this great picture of Kira. Every mother tries to train their child not to do this and I was trying hard. You can see about how far I was getting....

too many items

There are those items, which cause flashbacks; they call us to years of yesterday where our memories are stored, waiting to be disturbed again. Those items which go unused in the humdrum of life… they are for our hearts.

Too many items, such as dresses, berets, bands, shoes, socks, tights, sweaters, sippie cups, flip-flops, toys, pj's, and dolls. I am trying to clean up the apartment. I have this problem that started a year and a half ago; I have all these items that no one wears, and yet I don't want to put them away. The tempting thought of giving them away is soon shut down when I realize I am attached to these items. I can't give these items away, nor can I pack them. Some days I think I will just take them to the clothing bank. After all, what good are things that no one uses? Especially when there is probably some little girl in the world with no clothes to wear. If mine died, then I could at least clothe a needy one somewhere with all these items. Something inside me rebels like a horse with the wrong bit. I want to turn the other way. It's just not right; I can't give away items that were once used by a little girl I love so much. It feels wrong. These items are part of my memories of yesterday. My heart hangs on to the tangible things that cause me to remember.

But the fact remains that they are in the way. Not because I can't find room for them, but because no one that I can see uses them. Their owner is gone from this earth. She will never use them again… and so I look at them. I move them around while convincing myself not to put them away and that our house has enough room for them. Today I cleaned up the hair drawer. It was full of clips and bands that haven't been used since February 19. I was relieved to not find any dark hairs this time. No one uses those clips. Anna doesn't like them nor does she have much hair. Marlea has lots of hair and so tends not to use many clips. I loved to buy clips for Kira, which can easily be told by the amount still in the drawer. One night at Wal-Mart I bought a big pack only to get home and realize that I had two, thanks to Marlea's hand reaching out sneakily into the rack. Somehow they all got put into the drawer too. They are still there, but no one uses them. Marlea seemed to stop months ago; no fun exists to only match yourself. There are lots of bands also. They seem to be too big for Anna and too small for Marlea. So I look at them again and organize them back into their space. Oh well, maybe sometime Anna will use them. I shrug as I feel the tears in my heart. Last week I cleaned up the drawers in their room. One drawer was full of dearly loved clothes. Too big for Anna, yet too small for Marlea. No one needs them but I carefully retrieved the ones that will soon fit Anna and stuffed the rest back in. Anna picked out the pair of ugliest pj's and claimed them proudly as her "balloons" since they have balloons printed on the fabric. The shoe drawer was tough because Kira loved shoes. I left the boots and some flip-flops, and put the rest away. It will be a long time yet until size ten fits Anna even though she is just nine months away from being as old as Kira. I skimmed over the sock-and-tights drawer; too many memories to face, and too many tights without an owner. Did she really wear all of these? I organized the sweaters and put several away. She also had a lot of them. Kira was a particular dresser at her age, and her sweaters carried some weight in her mind. But again, it will be a long time until little Anna can wear 4T. What was Kira doing wearing 4T at age 2 anyhow, I wonder?

I go into the laundry where I keep the girls' dresses and just sigh. It's hopeless. I can't bear to touch them. Anna should have her dresses there instead of the little closet, but oh well, it will do for now. The pain of moving the ones in the laundry is too great, so I proceed to make the little closet more usable. Will these dresses ever fit Anna? Seems light-years away. 5T and 6T? It will be years if they ever will correctly fit Anna. Too little for Marlea, too big for Anna, yet they stay there. They remind me of the life that used to be… of the person I miss. I will let myself hang onto them, to the memories I treasure in my heart.

Forget it, I am also leaving the toys out that aren't used. I will just move around them and smile, wishing someone would play with them and I would have to pick them up. Some of the dolls were banished to the basement, but the ones she played with the most still float uselessly around the house. Some days they are played with and some days they are not. No one is really dedicated to their care, but I like to pick them up and put them away. Forget the stuffed animals too, and the extra pillow in the bed. They can just stay there!

Kira loved to be combed but she hated having her hair in ponytails, if that makes any sense. She had this disobedient circle of hair to the side of her hairline. On the other side was a swath of hair that was equally disobedient. It was too short for the ponytails, too short for braids, and too fine for clips. It was just long enough to hang in her eyes, and of course, in her food. So I would sometimes clip it back with two clips. She was great at losing them. We still found one this year in the yard. That disobedient swath of hair now resides in Merlin's suit-coat pocket. Maybe it will always stay there. I am not in a hurry to get it out.

raindrops

Raindrops on roses and whiskers on kittens, snowflakes that stay on my nose and eyelashes, brown paper packages tied up with strings, these are a few of my favorite things. When the dog bites, when the bee stings, when I am feeling sad, I simply remember my favorite things and then I don't feel so bad. "A Sound of Music"

Something mysterious is happening to me. I feel myself coming out of the clouds and emerging into light. It has been a gradual process since passing the year mark of Kira's death. Some days it calls me from a mighty mountain; some days from the valley. I listen to it intently. Some days I climb the mountain with giant steps, ready to conquer. Some days the tears slip as I take teeny steps in the valley. Other days I might skip on the level ground halfway between in a rather hesitant motion. Some days the skips on level ground are intermittent with a regular walk as I embrace the new normal. Still other days my heart dares me to be normal to stay on this regular walk…but my body isn't ready so I fluctuate.

The past several weeks the feeling has grown stronger, partly due to an experience one of my close friends is having. It's a friend I love dearly, who as a child befriended me with cute loving notes that encouraged me despite the ten-year age difference between us. As the years went by our friendship became stronger and we spent some time together each month. After she graduated from high school she worked for me for several years. Last year when Kira lost consciousness here at home, she was working here and was the first one to come into the house. She gathered up Marlea and Anna and took them out of the apartment. Her presence that day was a great relief to me, and yet I felt so badly that she had to see that amount of pain. On the other hand, she felt as if she were giving an immeasurable gift. This time I really needed her. In the months that followed, our relationship dwindled, partly due to her being gone for several months and partly due to my lack of energy.

Now, she is having a difficult experience. I feel a fervor rising up inside of me to give…it's the kind of giving that it close to my heart. It's a gift that simply requires time and words of empathy, encouragement. Strangely, the very one that I wanted to shield from my pain now listens to my words of encouragement. I don't need to explain how desperate and out of control I was; she knows, she saw me. I was thinking all these things after visiting her. It was raining and I was sad.

I was partly sad also because my next stop was at Hershey hospital to visit another friend whose child had meningitis. The raindrops fell faster along with my tears as I turned my van toward Hershey on 322. I was nervous and angry at the same time. I didn't want to go back there. I was by myself; I had no cushion on which to lean and I was going to have to walk in there all alone. The sun briefly came out and I wished for a rainbow. "God maybe then I could see and know again that You love me" I thought to myself.

I arrived at Hershey with my heart still pounding and anger simmering. Why does God let some children die and others live, anyhow? I pondered as I dove into a parking spot far away from the main entrance. I decided to walk off my feelings. Alas, I reached the door and I was still in shambles. The lady at the registration told me the child was on the seventh floor. Yes, unfortunately I would have to walk down that forbidden hallway. I wanted to scream "God I can't do this. I have to have someone to walk with me!" My memories of this hallway cause my mind to revert to several months ago. I see us, the heartbroken parents stumbling down that hallway for the last time. It was almost midnight when we left the hospital that night of the 24th of February. We were more tired than words could ever express. But our broken hearts dreaded the next days and what we knew lay ahead of us. We also knew our little girl would be wheeled out this hallway with the undertaker. We, in turn, would go outside to our van and to her empty car seat. The grief that hallway holds in our memories, and now God was asking me to walk down it alone and visit a child who was going to live?

I stepped off the elevator and signed in at the desk. Tears blurred my eyes as I wrote down my name. Step by step I forced myself to walk along the hall. This must be called facing one's fears, my mind tells me. My determination jumps into the front seat as I reach the patient's doorway and yes, she is sitting up in bed smiling. My heart flip-flops. In a way it's nice to know children can recover from meningitis, the viral kind, I learn as we talk. By the time our visit was over, my happiness for them outweighed my anger and nervousness. I left the room feeling as if I had done the right thing by visiting. I cheered them up, but probably more importantly than that I was feeling triumphant for just being okay with being in this place. As I turned and walked the hall again thoughts went through my head like "God please just don't let any of my children ever need to be here again." But it does not look as if everyone dies that comes here.

I felt as if I had accomplished something as I opened my car door. It was raining again but this time I was thinking "Somewhere in all this pain and grief there are answers." Maybe even beauty. Maybe I am and will become a more true example of God. Maybe God is using my own pain to enable me to understand others' pain more. Yes, I do care more. Admitting that simple fact finally made sense to me. Suffering has deepened my understanding of the cross like never before. Grasping the possibility that I can be more like Jesus through all this? I passed a sign that seems to me to read mockingly "Hershey—the sweetest place on earth." I grimace, harrumph; maybe to some. Really, I felt like tearing down the sign or at least putting holes through the word "sweetest". Fortunately I was taught to not always do what I felt.

As I drive on through the rain my mind reverts again to the power of Christ in me and living redemptively. Suddenly the clouds break and the sun shines through the rain. I look around anxiously for my rainbow and find none. Just raindrops, sun, and clouds. Selfishly I ask God why He can't give me a rainbow when I think I need one. About five minutes later I think I see some color. No, I must be imagining things. But no, it really is! In front of me emerged a beautiful rainbow. I sat humbly swallowing all my selfish thoughts and in turn became amazed at God. Okay God, I get it. I am actually as small and ugly as a raindrop. It's through your Light in my life that I can become beautiful. You can even use the back part of my raindrop; the ugly painful experiences I have had; the grief-filled days; the heartbreaking, agonizing minutes to bend a second time and create more color. Maybe sometime I will even see a double rainbow in my life. That will have to wait, because for now I only see a single one in front of me. The rain might continue to fall but God's light in my life will still make beautiful color. I savored the rainbow; soon I noticed people braking. The traffic came to a halt and for the next ten minutes God left the rainbow for me to see. I had lots of time to soak in the love of God.

I enjoyed these explanations:

Rainbows appear when raindrops (similar to a prism) reflect sunlight, thus breaking white sunlight into colors.

How is light reflected to create rainbows?

As light enters a water droplet, the different wavelength colors bend at slightly separate angles. Some of this light reflects off the back of the droplet and is bent a second time as the light beam emerges from the droplet. Drops at different angles send distinctively different colors to the eye.

If light is hitting raindrops at a proper angle, a secondary, larger rainbow will appear outside of the main rainbow. This secondary rainbow is fainter in color than the main one because the light has been reflected twice by each raindrop. This double reflection also reverses the colors in the secondary rainbow.

To see a rainbow, an observer must have the back to the sun and rain must be falling in some part of the sky. Since each raindrop is lit by the white light of the sun, a spectrum of colors is produced.

No two observers will ever witness exactly the same rainbow, because each will view a different set of drops at a slightly different angle. Also, each color seen is from different raindrops.

When Kira was five months old she wiggled around on the floor like a fish. One day I was snipping beans outside and left the door open slightly. Before I could react she had wiggled out onto the porch and down over the threshold. I was a bit astounded. That was one of her first moves that proved she loved going outside.

bowl hat

A simple bowl intended for basic use, becoming a security accessory and necessity during flu season and grief. As upside-down as life had become, so bowl also went upside down as a hat, hiding feelings inside.

In the winter of 2009 we had the flu bug. Instead of buckets we use bowls to catch the spillage. Marlea and Kira had matching bowls, one bigger than the other. Over the time of Kira's death, Marlea became fiercely attached to her bowl. She named it "Bowl Hat." The days visiting in the hospital she always brought it along, often on her head. In the days, weeks, and months that followed, she and "bowl hat" were inseparable. It slept beside her at night, was carried around during the day, went to Grandma's house, and went everywhere in the van. She would have even taken it into church if we would have allowed her to do so. Convincing her to go to kindergarten without it was a chore. I relented several days and allowed the hat to ride along in the backpack. It went with us to El Salvador stuffed into the carry-on. It traveled to Ohio at Christmas, and to Ohio again in May.

I would try to make her leave it at home but was only wasting energy. The bowl hat seemed to be a vital part of her life, which connected her to the loss she was experiencing from losing her playmate. She was determined, so eventually I accepted it as part of our family for however long it wanted

227

to stay. Often the bowl hat was used for its intended purpose and saved me from a wild dash for something else handy to grab. Many a night it saved the bed and floor from a mess. Marlea is a little "feeler" and many times it just gave some security that was missing in her life from all the trauma. About eight months ago we found reasons for the stomach issues for Marlea. Daily enzymes decreased the need for the repeated use of the "bowl hat." However, it was still a very important object. I became really tired of looking at that thing all over our apartment so I started sticking it under the bed at opportune moments. Always it would come back out again and as a reward I would receive glares for my actions. A few months ago it started staying under the bed for longer periods of time. But anytime there was more stress around, back out it would come. It was still a must-have on vacations.

Last weekend we went on a trip; we left on Saturday and came home on Tuesday. We took a camper to distract us from the fact of our first vacation since Kira's death that didn't include extended family. It proved to be a good distraction. On Monday I kept thinking that something was missing. I couldn't pinpoint it. Later, as I was cleaning up the camper the thought suddenly struck me. "Bowl Hat" was missing. It was still under the bed at home! Tears filled my eyes as I grasped what was happening in my daughter's heart. To heal means freedom from nerves, which in turn heals the stomach, which eliminates the need for "bowl hat." I remained quiet, and we actually returned home; and "bowl hat" was still under the bed. It might need to come out again sometimes and I am okay with that. I might even like to see it sometimes. But mostly I choose to embrace the fact of a little heart that is healing, nerves that are calming down, and a stomach that doesn't heave. In its place I see snatches of the little girl I used to know. She is sweet, helpful, and plays nicely with her little sister. The sad eyes with circles around them are gone, and the sparky ones are coming back. The food is disappearing off her plate again and reappearing on her torso. Her happiness and freedom from the bondage of "bowl hat" also allow my mind to lessen its worrisome thoughts about her.

Our last family vacation was spent in Louisville, Kentucky visiting the Horse Park. The girls loved it, as did their parents. They had life-size, pretend horses to ride. The horses galloped, neighed, and even reared a little. This picture of Kira reminds me of the white horses she rides freely in heaven.

perspective

Then he answered and spake unto me, saying, This [is] the word of the LORD unto Zerubbabel, saying, Not by might, nor by power, but by my spirit, saith the LORD of hosts. **Zechariah 4:6**

I have become different. I cannot detour around that truth. Grief and pain have changed me and my perspectives on life. A few weeks ago, my cousin was killed in Afghanistan. He and nine others were part of a mobile eye clinic in a remote part of the country. They were ambushed, robbed, and killed. A week and a half later we attended his memorial service. During that time I found myself unable to properly grieve and mourn his death. In fact, I was thoroughly confused.

Sunday at his memorial service I was finally able to cry. Then the tears came in torrents, and I was out of control. Days later I decided I still haven't really mourned his death. My longing to enter heaven has stolen and replaced what would have been my feelings of grief for the loss of his life. Yes, that envy has stolen my ability to grieve. Why would I grieve my own loss when he is experiencing heaven? I want to go there…not that I want to leave my loved ones, but my desire for heaven is burning. The small taste God gave me the night Kira died will stay with me forever. The peace heaven gives and the feeling of everything being perfect; no more worries, cares, strife, war, arguments, or different opinions about life. My perspective on death has changed. I always grieved for my loss of connection with that person. I still do to some extent. Now, my grief is more associated with the living and the pain they will endure until heaven can be real for them. My tears at the memorial service were for my aunt, uncle, and their family. I still have some balancing to do; I am still partially confused.

A few nights later I had a dream. Glen and I were on a hillside. There were steps on the slight hillside and gardens. He and I were walking along a path that was beautifully landscaped. As we were standing there a tricycle came crashing past us, down the steps, and landed with a bang in the flowerbed. It had no rider and seemed to come from nowhere. I perceived the crash to be a disaster and was upset about it. The trike was mangled and demolished beyond repair. Oddly, it didn't seem to matter to anyone except us that the tricycle had crashed. One would think that there would have been a hurt child or at least an upset one around; but no, it was just us and the tricycle. Glen didn't have much to say but I had the feeling right away that he expected me to put it back together. I was definitely connected to this three-wheeled piece of metal. I was totally annoyed. After all, it's a messed up tricycle! What was I supposed to do with it? It seemed to me to be impossible and ridiculous. The only thing he had to say was "Be careful how you try to put it back together."

There were other words that I don't remember; probably because I couldn't grasp them. His perspective on the situation was so different than mine. Mine was so sarcastic that his positive one fell on deaf ears. As if I would even try to put a tricycle back together? I am the type of person that is much more gifted at taking things apart; don't even ask me to put batteries in a baby monitor. I always forget which way they go in and mess around with it for a while. Completely opposite of my husband, who can fix almost anything. Still, the feeling is so powerful in my mind. Us, standing there together staring down the steps at this mangled piece of metal. And he thought I could fix it. Totally ridiculous. Glen was eight years older than I. I always looked up to him and his opinion really mattered to me.

When Kira died he was in Afghanistan but he wrote about how he spent the day crying and meditating. The death was so hard on him that his colleagues suggested he go home for a while. His own nieces and nephews are close in age to my children, so it really hit home for him. Vividly I recall in my dream searching his face, trying to figure out why in the world he would think that I could fix this tricycle. Somehow something about this he understood and I obviously didn't. Glen was naturally more laid back than I am. He seemed to have an eternal view on this tricycle that I just could not get a hold of. I realized in my dream that it was a real privilege for me to be standing there with him since I knew that he had died. I felt totally dumbfounded.

I awakened to my crazy thoughts and realized the dream was not real and I was still lying in my bed here in Lancaster County. Outside my window the weeds were growing and the unheavenly beetles were eating my flowers. But the feeling still hasn't left me; it lingers on waiting to be figured out. The feeling that he believed I could fix that mangled tricycle; certainly a different perspective than I had of my own abilities. My own life feels mangled just like the tricycle. Could it be that it was my life, me that came crashing down the steps in that beautifully landscaped flowerbed? Is it me that is in shambles, ruined in my eyes beyond repair? Do I look at myself and think that I will never be back to what I consider normal? Is it me that is trying to be put back together? I do feel like a demolished piece of metal twisted beyond recognition by the grief and pain in my life.

And yes, it is definitely me that is trying to be careful how I put this all back together. Yes, I feel called, maybe even commanded to put this back together and be a usable person in God's kingdom. I will always be a little twisted. You may still wonder in ten years when you meet me what "crash" occurred in my life. By the grace of God my three wheels, body, soul, and spirit will come together again. Through the power of God I will ride life's journey again joyfully pedaling my way closer to Jesus. The spirit of the Lord will guide my steering, my spirit and give my soul enough sustenance to stay on the seat of life.

This dream was crazy; a message from Glen simply stating in regular language that he believes my life can be pieced back together. I just have to wonder what all goes on in heaven. Did Glen want to tell me that before he died and so God let me have the dream? Another one of those questions I have for Him when I reach those pearly gates…but wait, will we remember our questions?

God also showed me in a funny way that other people's perspectives are different than mine. It broadened my horizon and allowed me to be more okay with however they would like to perceive me. Last week, when we were walking out of a restaurant Marlea and Anna were ahead of me. I must have looked tired. A kind looking middle-aged couple was outside eating ice cream. The man was watching the girls. He looked at me and said, "I bet they are a handful." The words were already coming out of my mouth to inform him that no they really are not but when there were three of them I was busy. I bit my tongue, smiled and replied, "Yes, they are." For the first time since Kira's death, I felt myself allow a person's perspective on our family to remain as it appears. In turn I felt God showing me that my perspective on death has changed and that is okay. But that is for me to feel and not everyone else. Each person grieves differently and for different reasons. My respect of those different reasons along with my respect for the Christian body of believers is growing.

Anna is learning to ride a bike with training wheels. She can barely reach the pedals now. Her eyes glisten with pride as I try to help her. They remind me so much of the same pride I saw in her sister as she learned to ride the bike. In Kira's eyes, she became Marlea's equal because she could ride bike also. For Anna, she is simply being proud of turning the pedals. I miss that fierce competition between Marlea and Kira. It made for crazy times….

reactions

Okay, how about I bounce you off of this wall and then when I am finished, you can bounce me off of that wall?

Reactions; we all have them. Reactions to people, circumstances, or something that just really sets us off. We are all different, so we all react in our own unique way. We even get demanding about needing space while we react. We spend time thinking of excuses for ourselves, or try to explain our way out of our own human-ness.

A few weeks ago in this house we all had our own reactions. The tombstone made its arrival by way of Merlin's truck. Marlea and Anna thought it was great to go with Daddy to pick up Kira's tombstone. I grimaced and my stomach turned at the thought of it being great to go pick up your sister's tombstone. I reacted by living out my sullen angry feelings. They were excited and proud of it; I was not. They tried to persuade me to go out and look at it in the truck; I did not want to see it in Merlin's truck. To me, the taste of death stinks and that is what the tombstone felt to me that day.

Later Merlin took it to the graveyard and laid it on the grave because he didn't have the correct material to put it in place. Finally on Sunday after church I could no longer deny that it belongs to me. I went and looked at it…sullenly, of course. I found Marlea lying on the stone with a smile on her face; I took only one glance and muttered that it's nice. Merlin was very gracious to me, giving me the space I needed to react to my feelings. He designed the tombstone himself, so it would have been nice to be receiving compliments instead of grimaces from his wife. He too was having his own reactions; only being a man it was the thing to do to put up the tombstone. Marlea kept asking me if I like it. "Yes" I replied, just not there! More like I wanted to yell "I hate it!" It could have been the most unique tombstone available on the face of the earth and I would still be grimacing and mad.

So I left and my family followed me to the van. I managed to tell Merlin that it is very nice. Anna had her own two-year old reaction by screaming life-threatening screams as we drove. To her the tombstone was part of our family, something we should take along, not leave in the graveyard. Why would we leave it in the graveyard after picking it up in Daddy's truck? She wanted to bring it home to our house. When we arrived home I was thinking on these things when Marlea came into the kitchen carrying her beloved "Bowl Hat." I was sure she was going to say that she is going to use it again. As I had written some time ago, it was under the bed. She handed it to me. "I don't need this anymore" she said. Words were trying to come out of my gaping mouth as I stared at her. Alas, I had no words for such a change. I had not expected to ever receive that bowl back. And here she was giving it to me after lying in the graveyard with her head on her deceased sister's tombstone. I took it, but was totally confused by the series of events. So that was the last thing for her, putting the tombstone over Kira's grave? To me the action brought reactions; nasty, ugly, sullen, angry ones. To my daughter it brought closure, peace, and acceptance. I felt slapped in the face.

So I thought about it, tried to talk about it with my friends, let myself be angry again. My mind played the "what if" games again as I struggled with God about giving back my daughter before I thought it was time. In the end I decided to accept the tombstone. After all, if I didn't, I would have to face my daughter's questions and probes for the next fifty years. Maybe acceptance was the easy way out but it surely did bring more peace. The next

Sunday I went to the graveyard again. Two of my friends went with me along with a group of Marlea's and Anna's friends. This time it was set upright in place and Marlea was riding it full of grins. It was easier this time and we all shed some tears. Acceptance was easier when I realized that it is not only painful for me to look at it, but also for others. As I gazed at it I realized that it is a really nice tombstone. It has her picture engraved, the Jesus Rock of Ages symbol similar to the picture on her blog, and her name. As I stared at it I also realized that we had forgotten to put "daughter of" onto the stone. But I don't really care. At least my name isn't there with hers. Somehow it eased the pain and I breathed a sigh of relief. The next Sunday I went again. Now it's less bitter. I feel okay about it. I still can't say that I like it, but I do say it's a nice tombstone, if ever such a thing were possible.

I seem to have had numerous other reactions. Anna is growing and is now two-and-a-half. She and Marlea are starting to actually play things that make sense together. Once again I hear little feet trotting after each other, someone hollering "Mia," and a little voice singing "God is Great" at the table before meals. It's nice, but I find myself being afraid of it. It reminds me too much of "how it used to be." I attempt to face the fear and remind myself that it's not a valid fear. The actual fear is simply the fear of Anna also being taken to heaven. I need not fear it because God is in control. If I really trust Him like I say I do, then it should not be a fear. But alas, I am human. My fear does not keep me from enjoying Anna's antics and play. I smile and thank God for the healing that we have experienced even if it means not thinking about the "hole" so much. I thank God also for Anna's vast vocabulary and how that makes it so much easier for her and Marlea to play and communicate.

I am also reacting to upcoming changes in our family. Baby four is due in several days. Good changes, but I miss the "Sunshine" girl who played such a vital part in our family. I realize that she would be helping me a lot with the baby, especially when Marlea is at school. She would also be playing with Anna. Instead Anna is making baby noises and screams in preparation for baby four's arrival. A few days ago I decided I had no other way to make room for baby four without putting some of Kira's clothes away. It was terribly hard to do, and still felt like betrayal almost two years later. Memories are still fresh in my mind. Anna reacted by standing in a corner and screaming. She made big bold statements like "Kira doesn't need this anymore because she is up in heaven." Or "Kira won't mind if I wear this because she is in heaven." Those words added to my pain, but the bluntness and truth she spoke also helped me keep in focus that it is simply the truth. Some of her clothes fit Anna, so I didn't need to put them all away. I freely admit that some clothes in Anna's drawer are quite oversized for her little self. Until Anna grows into them, they still belong to Kira.

And so the famous "Bowl Hat" has become part of my kitchen utensils again. Sterilized and scrubbed, it sits redeemed in the drawer in the bottom of my oven. Back in its familiar surroundings, it thanks God for the journey. Bowl Hat's world was really broadened on this journey. Every morning I take it out and beat our eggs in it, scrambling them for my family's breakfast. Later I wash it, dry it, and carefully stow it back under the oven. As I do it calls me to embrace the reality of today joyfully. It's just a common-looking bowl, but one with which I will never part. I am thankful for the ability to use the bowl and not keep shoving it under the bed. This "Bowl Hat" is a symbol to me of the blessings this journey has, is, and will be yet in the future. And yes, this bowl will soon be mixing another egg for the additional member coming to our family, bringing with him more healing, enabling me to trust my Jesus more again.

mountain top

Without the valley, there would be no mountain. It's the view from the top that makes the valley look beautiful.

Two years ago today our three-year-old lost her breath in front of me… right here in this room. I watched, horrified, as I realized that she was not going to start breathing on her own. Panic threatened to overtake me as I frantically tried to remember how to start CPR. Seconds later I was on the bathroom floor yelling at the 911 operator to help me remember what to do and how. That horrific moment, among others, still stands out in my mind. That was only the beginning of the valley. Minutes later my neighbor (an EMT) rushed in and together we worked to revive Kira. The ambulance crew soon arrived and took over attempting to stabilize her. As I reached for the phone and called my sister I could feel my panic and adrenaline being replaced with fear as I yelled into the phone "Kira is dying." The words seemed to rush out of my mouth and chill everything around. What seemed like hours (in reality, only a few minutes) later I watched through blurred eyes as the ambulance sped out of our driveway with Kira in the back and her daddy seated in the front. Time seemed to stop as I tried to collect myself and go to the hospital. Life became a mad cycle of running to the hospital, feeding the baby, and trying to stay collected the next five days. My fears became valid and I confronted them as the fifth day came and we said good-bye to Kira as she peacefully slipped from this world into the next... And then this journey of relearning my trust in God.

A year ago we had a party. A celebration party of Kira's life here and in heaven. Somehow I felt God calling me to celebrate with my whole heart. Even harder was the call to celebrate other people's children amidst the pain of losing my own. The past year had been very difficult for us and I was starting to feel as if we were coming out of the gutter. Merlin had been sick for months. In August Anna sprained her ankle and I had a miscarriage. It was just the beginning of my downward journey. I was simply worn out. I was rescued from my coming crash (better interpreted a nervous breakdown) by our doctor, although I will say that the drugs are still in the cabinet, unopened. I keep them there to remind myself how close I was to an emotional breakdown. By February and the year mark we were all on the healing road. The party was good; it felt okay to celebrate Kira's heaven date. Plus the amazing support we felt from everyone that came to celebrate with us was also very healing. In the weeks that followed I continued to feel healing and a release of my own will.

Weeks later we were pleasantly surprised to realize that we were expecting a baby. We simply did not expect it. Not opposed, we both really wanted another child, especially Marlea, who had prayed fervently every day since Kira's death. The pictures on her door strongly alluded to her heart's desire. The next months were difficult for me as I grappled with grieving and being joyful about the baby. Joy and sadness seem to be at opposite ends of the spectrum. I wasn't quite up to it physically. That combined with the hot summer had me mainly exhausted most days.

So it happened that on November 11, 2010 we welcomed Brent Jaxon into the world. It was a calm, fairly uneventful delivery (as much as childbirth can be.) Minutes later as I lay holding our son I suddenly realized that I am lying in a hospital bed holding a baby. My mind flashed back to the night at Hershey holding Kira as her heart beat its last. Instinctively in my head I compared it to now, holding a new baby. Amazement filled my heart. Earlier the nurse had been asking about our family and I had shared a little about Kira. Now they were asking more questions. I suddenly realized I was lying in this bed all this time and didn't even think about the bed similarity until now. As I talked with them more, they shared my grief with tears and more questions. But strangely I wasn't crying. A feeling rose up inside of me, a feeling of being okay with everything. Yes, here I was, okay. It seemed like part of my life, a life that was mine. Weeks earlier God had told me that I would have an experience through Brent's birth that would be a mountaintop. This was my mountaintop. I could feel it, I literally felt on the top; even viewing the valley from the top. Praise filled me for the faithfulness of God. Yes, that valley; yes, this mountaintop. But it would not be a mountaintop without the valley. I gazed in gratefulness at our son Brent, whose name means "mountaintop."

No, we didn't try to name him that because of thinking it's going to be a mountaintop. When Kira was in the womb we thought she might be a boy. To be safe, we found a boy name we liked. Obviously we didn't need it. When Anna was born we kept it on the back shelf again just in case. When we found out that this baby was to be a boy, we somewhat automatically named him Brent. We didn't even realize that the name meant mountaintop. We just liked the name.

The power of that experience carried me through the next weeks. I missed Kira tremendously. The combination of adjusting to a baby, hormonal changes that come with birth, and the Christmas season proved to be a terrible combination for me. Merlin was also dealing with changes except that men tend to retreat, which only made my pain worse. Many days I felt as if I could hardly go on...then the real-ness of my mountaintop experience would come back. It wouldn't bring me out of my sorrow, but it did convince me that sometime I will be okay again. It was the taste of the "feeling" that kept my head up.

When Brent was three weeks old he was having difficulty breathing. I took him to the doctor and then for a chest x-ray; his chest was clear. A few nights later I awakened to the sensation that something was wrong. I jumped out of bed, paranoid. His head was cold but he was breathing, although labored. I was just downright scared. Fear came crawling into my heart that God would give us a son and then take him away again. He was better after his feeding but I held him the rest of the night. And yes, one could have guessed; it was the weekend so into the ER we went. I couldn't believe it. Us, here again. It's like God just wants us to be okay with going there and facing our fears. I wasn't too surprised with the whole ordeal. God had told me a while ago that something would happen with Brent to help me learn to trust Him more. I pretended it was my imagination… but then I knew I had heard it.

Yes, I did learn to trust Him more through it but in a different way than with all the other episodes. I felt like God was simply calling me to face my fear, maybe even confront my feeling of helplessness. I learned a lot more about conquering my fear simply because I had something to do. Kira's death left me with a terrible feeling that there is nothing to do. God showed me through the experience with Brent that often just a simple something takes care of the problem; it's not always a dramatically complicated outcome. In his case a nebulizer treatment was everything necessary. We did it several times at home for a few weeks afterward, and he has been fine since. He just couldn't move the mucous. Or maybe God just wants us to walk into the ER so often we don't even think it strange anymore?

Christmas came and went. Lots of feelings again, mostly sad. Strangely, Marlea was sick for about two weeks again right before Christmas, and somewhat added to my loss of sanity. I can't say I do really well with all of the above on a pile. The one day, I took Marlea for a doctor appointment; I made the appointment at one place and went to another location. They looked at me as if I might be a little shady. I just smiled and said, "Well, I guess I am still post-partum." I was glad for the excuse. "Here, give my daughter a fix so I can get my sanity back again" is what I was thinking. It was nice to look back on Christmas day and feel the difference between last Christmas and this Christmas. This past one was definitely easier for all of us. I still keenly felt the desire to be joyful on Christmas but it is so difficult when not everyone was here, and never will be again on this earth. We tried to distract ourselves, but I can't say it worked really well. At midnight after I had finally convinced Brent to settle down I was exhausted, worn out emotionally and physically. I cried and cried, then went to bed and slept. The next day I awoke, and Christmas was past and the world looked brighter. In fact, ever since then the world has been looking brighter again. I feel as if I am finally accepting Kira's death.

In turn I am blessed with a peace unknown to me previously. I feel real joy. I was raised in a Christian home and taught to be obedient to God and to accept the circumstances He brings into our lives. Not accepting Kira's death to me felt so disobedient and hypocritical. I knew I had to fight through it because I couldn't deny the obvious, nor ignore the grief cycle if I wanted to heal. To accept the grief stages took patience and trust that my wounded heart would heal and I would feel peaceful again. I feel it coming. I've been told I look happy again. I am amazed how much better I am feeling physically. The muscle bunchies leave me the whole way some days and I have a lot more energy. It just takes lots of energy to grieve!

A few observations from the last three months:

What can be done with a little girl who thinks turning three will make her die? She doesn't want to go to Jesus, she says.

I look at Brent; he will never know Kira on earth. That seems wrong because they are both part of our family.

We have lived two years without Kira. Next year it will be as long without her as with her.

As a mother, wisdom and thoughtfulness are required to remember to ask the seven-year-old every several days what she is thinking and to purposely spend time with her, reflecting on her feelings about Kira and her death. Unfortunately, though I am her mother, I am human and not perfect.

Men and women still grieve differently.

Anna turns three in April. Her actions and antics somewhat remind me of Kira and how much I was enjoying her. After she turns three, I will be reminded constantly of what I lost with Kira.

I still fear someone I love being taken from me…then I am reminded of the definition of "mine."

God has unique ways of making me stronger.

God's timing is always right.

God gave us a visible sign to help us remember the mountaintop.

Brent is God's sign to Marlea that He heard her prayer. She says "I wanted Kira to live; she died. Then God gave us Brent!"

Life and death are so opposite. Likewise the feelings that go with them are opposed.

I live in awe of a God who gives and a God who takes away. In times of doubt, I am learning to trust.

When Anna was born, Kira was simply overbearing. I have many pictures of her bending over Anna, who is screaming hysterically. The only peace we could have seemed to be when they both had their pacifiers; to Kira they were then equal. We have the same scenario again. Only this time Anna is overbearing and Brent is screaming. Why don't babies like two-year-olds? It must be that fear of the unknown.

CHAPTER SIXTY-NINE

treasure

For where your treasure is, there shall your heart be also. **Luke 12:34**

I drive away from the traffic light in town and turn to drive up a hill. My car is revving, since this is a long hill. I press the gas a little harder, because I need to get finished with this errand as quickly as possible. At home a little boy is sleeping, and the babysitter is with him. He will want his mama before too long. My mind drifts to thoughts of the last days. This whole thing of being a mother to a little tyke is lots of work. I am reminded that I have done this four times now. Each time has been well worth it. Well, let's just say that I am still doing it with two of them, but I see the results a little more than can be seen at eight weeks old.

Then the thought hits me: I did all this work for three years with Kira and I have absolutely nothing to show for it. As a vapor, she is gone, untouchable to my aching arms. Flashbacks hit me; the painful act of childbirth, the hours of feeding a baby, the art of teaching her to eat, simply stuffing food in so that growth can occur, and the sleepless nights. Later on helping Kira learn to crawl, balance, and finally walk. In Kira's case many footsteps were taken to chase after her after she did learn to walk. So many things, so much time, and enormous amounts of energy only to have it pass before me at age three. The very age a child becomes more independent and self-sufficient. Instead of being able to enjoy it…I buried her. That body I cared for is underneath the sod! Anger stirs inside of me and I rev my car more, passing the next car up this long hill. And I am crazy enough to do this all a fourth time and dare to believe that he will be mine to keep? I want life to be stable, predictable. Once you give them to me, God, I am not giving You any more back.

I arrive at my destination. I am delivering dishes for a friend who brought us a meal. She wonders how I am. "Good" I lie. Where are the children? "With the babysitter" I reply. It is threatening snow and in the single digits; too cold for a baby to be outside. My friend is kind and caring; she asks more questions and we talk a bit.

I feel softened by the Godly interaction. Once more a person has drawn me to God by simple loving words.

Later on that night while trying to teach the baby to sleep, I am interrupted again by my own thoughts. The next several days I mulled them around in my head. Memories continued to stir me of all the time and effort I put into Kira's three years. Loss and so much disappointment. Dreams that will never take place. Experiences in life that will never be mine to enjoy. I continued to stir the pot.

A week or so later I was still thinking similarly. Suddenly and maybe even gradually everything began to make sense. I have this deep longing inside of me for God; to see the face of my heavenly Father. But in front of all this is a secret. It's the weird thing that I feel rather embarrassed about. Correctly, as a Christian I desire to see God. But there is piece of me in heaven calling persistently every day. Just as an earthly child calls her mother, so this child is calling me very clearly. Since Kira is a physical part of me, I intensely desire to see her as soon as I get to heaven. I even picture her in the whiteness just like in my visit to heaven that night. My view of heaven starts there, because I can only picture my child's face. I didn't see Jesus' face, so naturally I long for the face I can envision. Is she now already leading me to Jesus? I am fortunate to have a tangible pull to heaven. The earthly cares of this world seem to fade….

We treasure our children instinctively whether the child was born to us, or if we have cared for one that has been entrusted to us. Just like I am now carefully watching Brent every day, hour and minute, I did that for Kira too. She is one of my treasures, though she isn't here bodily.

Sunday morning weeks later, after our arrival at church we had a short devotional in the main auditorium, then split into different classes. I was a part of an upstairs Sunday school class. The room is off to the side, small and simple with brown walls, rose carpet and dinghy windows. Our group of about ten ladies sat in a circle. The teacher talked about heaven and our desire to go there. Suddenly I felt a crazy bottomless longing again like a surge of electricity inside me. I long to go there! I feel my brain embracing the fact that yes, Kira is my treasure; why shouldn't I long to go there? Three of my treasures are here on the earth, so naturally I long to be here as well. Both desires are correct and okay. The pull for heaven will not lessen with age. It is part of the journey this wound has brought in my life. It has refocused me, my actions, my thoughts, and the importance of life here, and will continue to do so. It is part of the "gift" healing has brought to me. No, I am not finished. On that day I stand before Jesus is the first time in my memory that I will be finished. Only then will I find the "missing piece" to my life. The wound, this scar will stay with me while here on this earth. Scarred by my own loss, I am unable to forget where my treasure is saved.

Then I wonder about this energy I feel. The energy is connecting other areas as well. The refocus going on in my heart and the powerful feeling of empathy for others in pain that I was unable to feel before is now evident. A strong desire has grown inside of me to love my children without reserve and more fully so they can better understand God. These things also must be part of the "gift" of healing. I hear older people talking about the beauty life's experiences can bring. This whole process mystifies me again. I can freely choose to live in the grace of God, no matter what life in this fallen world may hold. God left a choice of growth versus stagnancy. The truth is that God always wins in the heart of a person turned toward him. What Satan deemed for evil, God can use to accomplish good. With care, patience, and time, the wounds from happenings can heal. Wounds may bring growth, wisdom, and change scar tissue into something beautiful to behold.

Spiritually, I again choose to live fully. Gently my longing to feel complete pulls me to the foot of the cross where I can experience fullness as well as possible here on this earth.

Physically I continue embracing the "treasures" God has entrusted into my care.

Emotionally I wipe the tears away and smile. I am still opening my gift, wrapped with my own pain.

I dare myself daily to:

Reach out.

Touch it.

To embrace it as part of my life.

For inside this gift lies abundant, joyful life not hindered by scars. I have found re-established trust in my heavenly Father and His ability to provide sufficient grace for my wound, pain, healing, and life with a scar. Inside this gift lies the energy to live abundantly in a world full of disappointment and broken dreams. This gift contains a scar that, defying human nature, is becoming beautiful through redemption.

Acknowledgements

To my sweet daughters, Marlea and Anna: you have travelled this journey so well with me. Your love and affection in those dark days gave me a reason to live. Your belief in my ability to write this book kept me going when I wanted to forget it.

Brent: the mystery of your birth, your name, and my own mountaintop is straight from God, and a tangible reminder to me of my re-established trust.

My big sister, Renita. You have been with me all my life. Thank you for the many days you made sure I was okay, even driving to my house if necessary. Embracing my pain with me, so strong and dedicated, always pointing me back to God in my distress. To my loving older sisters: I could always feel your hearts here with me. To my big brother Arlin and my little brother, John: your compassion for me was so soft and tender on those dark days. Thanks to my faithful family for stoutly remaining by our sides through the ups and downs of this journey.

The title of this book I owe to my father. The security Dad offered me as a child paved the way for me to trust my heavenly Father and believe the redemption He has to offer me. His gigantic rough hands held mine on many a day as a child, so it feels right to have his hands holding the daisy on the cover.

To my mother for her steady presence in my life and in the lives of my children: your care still deeply touches my heart. You have encouraged me to walk this journey with caution. The warmth and love you offer me, your own grief with the loss of your grandchild, and the helplessness you experienced watching us grieve have strengthened my resolve to mother my own children well.

To the faithful Yutzy brothers: whether you knew it or not, you rescued us from despair more than once. The strength you offered us and the girls was revitalizing. To Mom and Dad Yutzy: thanks for your stability and encouragement.

Life would be desolate without you, Lydia. Your support and love through all my ideas, crazy or levelheaded, in this journey of grief and pain. Through every stage you have willingly embraced it with me.

To Dr. B: your illustrations of a wound aided my understanding of what was going on inside me emotionally and physically. Your understanding of the process grief takes on a physical body helped Merlin and I give each other room to grieve. Thank you for taking time to care for all of us on those dark days.

To my ever-faithful mentor Barb Kauffman: your presence in my life calmed many a raging battle. The experience of losing your own daughter became a blessing for me in your ability to understand my feelings before I spoke them. Being with you always convinced me that someday I will more clearly see God's redemption in my life.

To our friends and church family: your tender care for us in our weakest moments and days was a picture of God himself.

About the Author

Mary Lou Yutzy is married to Merlin Yutzy and the mother of four children, three on Earth and one in heaven. She grew up on a farm working in the garden, chasing calves, riding pony, and listening to croaking frogs for bedtime music. She attended a private school with grades one through twelve. Most days you will find her cooking, washing, cleaning, and caring for her family. She and her husband also operate Olde Homestead Suites, a small B&B in Lancaster County, Pennsylvania. She enjoys blessing people by offering good food, clean rooms, and a relaxing Christian atmosphere. Her desire is to be an encourager for God through finding joy in any moment, whether good or otherwise. For more about Wounded Trust visit www.woundedtrust.net

CPSIA information can be obtained at www.ICGtesting.com
Printed in the USA
LVOW061323080612

285276LV00002B/1/P